# PROJECT CHECO SOUTHEAST ASIA REPORT

**GROUP-1**
Excluded from automatic downgrading and declassification.

Published by Books Express Publishing
Copyright © Books Express, 2010
ISBN 978-1-907521-98-0
To purchase copies at discounted prices please contact
info@books-express.com

AFCSAMI-S 693978
6910102

**AIR FORCE EYES ONLY**

Declassified IAW E.O. 12958 by the
Air Force Declassification Office and
Approved for Public Release.
Date: 8-15-06

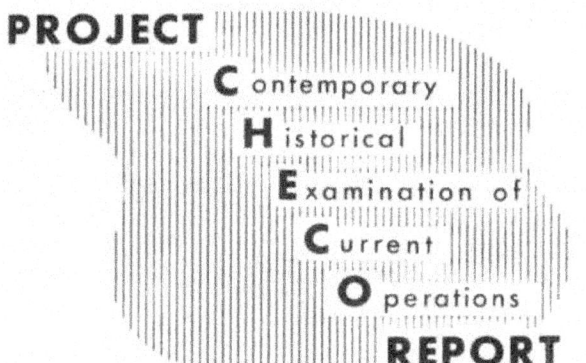

PROJECT
**C**ontemporary
**H**istorical
**E**xamination of
**C**urrent
**O**perations
REPORT

# TACTICAL AIRLIFT OPERATIONS

## 30 JUNE 1969

**HQ PACAF**
**Directorate, Tactical Evaluation**
**CHECO Division**

Prepared by:
MAJ DAVID R METS
Project CHECO 7th AF, DOAC

**AIR FORCE EYES ONLY**

PROJECT CHECO REPORTS

The counterinsurgency and unconventional warfare environment of Southeast Asia has resulted in the employment of USAF airpower to meet a multitude of requirements. The varied applications of airpower have involved the full spectrum of USAF aerospace vehicles, support equipment, and manpower. As a result, there has been an accumulation of operational data and experiences that, as a priority, must be collected, documented, and analyzed as to current and future impact upon USAF policies, concepts, and doctrine.

Fortunately, the value of collecting and documenting our SEA experiences was recognized at an early date. In 1962, Hq USAF directed CINCPACAF to establish an activity that would be primarily responsive to Air Staff requirements and direction, and would provide timely and analytical studies of USAF combat operations in SEA.

Project CHECO, an acronym for Contemporary Historical Examination of Current Operations, was established to meet this Air Staff requirement. Managed by Hq PACAF, with elements at Hq 7AF and 7AF/13AF, Project CHECO provides a scholarly, "on-going" historical examination, documentation, and reporting on USAF policies, concepts, and doctrine in PACOM. This CHECO report is part of the overall documentation and examination which is being accomplished. Along with the other CHECO publications, this is an authentic source for an assessment of the effectiveness of USAF airpower in PACOM.

MILTON B. ADAMS, Major General, USAF
Chief of Staff

# DEPARTMENT OF THE AIR FORCE
HEADQUARTERS PACIFIC AIR FORCES
APO SAN FRANCISCO 96553

REPLY TO
ATTN OF: DOTEC

30 June 1969

SUBJECT: Project CHECO Report, "Tactical Airlift Operations" (U)

SEE DISTRIBUTION PAGE

1. Attached is a SECRET document. It shall be transported, stored, safeguarded, and accounted for in accordance with applicable security directives. Each page is marked according to its contents. Retain or destroy in accordance with AFR 205-1. Do not return.

2. This letter does not contain classified information and may be declassified if attachment is removed from it.

FOR THE COMMANDER IN CHIEF

*[signature]*

WARREN H. PETERSON, Colonel, USAF
Chief, CHECO Division
Directorate, Tactical Evaluation
DCS/Operations

1 Atch
Proj CHECO Rprt (S), 30 Jun 69

# DISTRIBUTION LIST

1. SECRETARY OF THE AIR FORCE

    a. SAFAA . . . . . . . . . 1
    b. SAFLL . . . . . . . . . 1
    c. SAFOI . . . . . . . . . 2

2. HEADQUARTERS USAF

    a. AFBSA . . . . . . . . . 1

    b. AFCCS
        (1) AFCCSSA . . . . . . 1
        (2) AFCVC . . . . . . . 1
        (3) AFCAV . . . . . . . 1
        (4) AFCHO . . . . . . . 2

    c. AFCSA
        (1) AFCSAG . . . . . . 1
        (2) AFCSAMI . . . . . . 1

    d. AFGOA . . . . . . . . . 2

    e. AFIGO
        (1) AFISI . . . . . . . 3
        (2) AFISP . . . . . . . 1

    f. AFMSG . . . . . . . . . 1

    g. AFNIN
        (1) AFNIE . . . . . . . 1
        (2) AFNINA . . . . . . 1
        (3) AFNINCC . . . . . . 1
        (4) AFNINED . . . . . . 4

    h. AFAAC . . . . . . . . . 1
        (1) AFAMAI . . . . . . 1

    i. AFODC . . . . . . . . . 1
        (1) AFOAP . . . . . . . 1
        (2) AFOAPS . . . . . . 1
        (3) AFOCC . . . . . . . 1
        (4) AFOCE . . . . . . . 1
        (5) AFOMO . . . . . . . 1

    j. AFPDC
        (1) AFPDPSS . . . . . . 1
        (2) AFPMDG . . . . . . 1
        (3) AFPDW . . . . . . . 1

    k. AFRDC
        (1) AFRDD . . . . . . . 1
        (2) AFRDQ . . . . . . . 1
        (3) AFRDR . . . . . . . 1
        (4) AFRDF . . . . . . . 1

    l. AFSDC
        (1) AFSLP . . . . . . . 1
        (2) AFSME . . . . . . . 1
        (3) AFSMS . . . . . . . 1
        (4) AFSPD . . . . . . . 1
        (5) AFSSS . . . . . . . 1
        (6) AFSTP . . . . . . . 1

    m. AFTAC . . . . . . . . . 1

    n. AFXDC
        (1) AFXDO . . . . . . . 1
        (2) AFXDOC . . . . . . 1
        (3) AFXDOD . . . . . . 1
        (4) AFXDOL . . . . . . 1
        (5) AFXOP . . . . . . . 1
        (6) AFXOSL . . . . . . 1
        (7) AFXOSN . . . . . . 1
        (8) AFXOSO . . . . . . 1
        (9) AFXOSS . . . . . . 1
        (10) AFXOSV . . . . . . 1
        (11) AFXOTR . . . . . . 1
        (12) AFXOTW . . . . . . 1
        (13) AFXOTZ . . . . . . 1
        (14) AFXOXY . . . . . . 1
        (15) AFXPD . . . . . . 6
            (a) AFXPPGS . . . . 3

3. MAJOR COMMANDS

   a. TAC

      (1) HEADQUARTERS
         (a) DO. . . . . . . . . 1
         (b) DPL . . . . . . . . 2
         (c) DOCC. . . . . . . . 1
         (d) DORQ. . . . . . . . 1
         (e) DIO . . . . . . . . 1

      (2) AIR FORCES
         (a) 12AF
            1. DORF . . . . . . 1
            2. DI . . . . . . . 1
         (b) 19AF(DI) . . . . . . 1
         (c) USAFSOF(DO) . . . . 1

      (3) AIR DIVISIONS
         (a) 831AD(DO) . . . . . 1
         (b) 832AD(DO) . . . . . 2
         (c) 833AD(DDO) . . . . . 1
         (d) 835AD(DO) . . . . . 1
         (e) 836AD(DO) . . . . . 2
         (f) 838AD
            1. DO . . . . . . . 1
         (g) 839AD(DO) . . . . . 2

      (4) WINGS
         (a) 1SOW(DO) . . . . . . 1
         (b) 4TFW(DO) . . . . . . 1
         (c) 23TFW(DOI) . . . . . 1
         (d) 27TFW(DOP) . . . . . 1
         (e) 33TFW(DOI) . . . . . 1
         (f) 64TFW(DO) . . . . . 1
         (g) 67TRW(C) . . . . . . 1
         (h) 75TRW(DO) . . . . . 1
         (i) 316TAW(DOP) . . . . 1
         (j) 317TAW(EX) . . . . . 1
         (k) 363TRW(DOC) . . . . 1
         (l) 464TAW(DO) . . . . . 1
         (m) 474TFW(TFOX) . . . . 1
         (n) 479TFW(DOF) . . . . 1
         (o) 516TAW(DOPL) . . . . 1
         (p) 4410CCTW(DOTR) . . . 1
         (q) 4510CCTW(DO16-I) . . 1
         (r) 4554CCTW(DOI) . . . 1

      (5) TAC CENTERS, SCHOOLS
         (a) USAFTAWC(DA) . . . . 2
         (b) USAFTARC(DID) . . . 2
         (c) USAFTALC(DCRL) . . . 1
         (d) USAFTFWC(CRCD) . . . 1
         (e) USAFSOC(DO) . . . . 1
         (f) USAFAGOS(DAB-C) . . 1

   b. SAC

      (1) HEADQUARTERS
         (a) DOPL . . . . . . . . 1
         (b) DPLF . . . . . . . . 1
         (c) DM . . . . . . . . . 1
         (d) DI . . . . . . . . . 1
         (e) OA . . . . . . . . . 1
         (f) HI . . . . . . . . . 1

      (2) AIR FORCES
         (a) 2AF(DICS) . . . . . 1
         (b) 8AF(C) . . . . . . . 1
         (c) 15AF(DOA) . . . . . 1

      (3) AIR DIVISIONS
         (a) 3AD(DO) . . . . . . 3

   c. MAC

      (1) HEADQUARTERS
         (a) MAOID . . . . . . . 1
         (b) MAOCO . . . . . . . 1
         (c) MAFOI . . . . . . . 1
         (d) MACOA . . . . . . . 1

      (2) AIR FORCES
         (a) 21AF(OCXI) . . . . . 1
         (b) 22AF(OCXI) . . . . . 1

      (3) AIR DIVISIONS
         (a) 322AD(DO) . . . . . 1

      (4) WINGS
         (a) 61MAWg
            1. OIN . . . . . . . 1
         (b) 62MAWg(OCXP) . . . . 1
         (c) 436MAWg(OCXC) . . . 1

                (d) 437MAWg(OCXI) . . . . 2
                (e) 438MAWg(OCXC) . . . . 1
                (f) 445MAWg
                    1. OC . . . . . . . . 1
                    2. WDO-PLI . . . . . . 1

            (5) MAC SERVICES
                (a) AWS(AWXW) . . . . . . 1
                (b) ARRS(ARXLR) . . . . . 1
                (c) ACGS(AGOV) . . . . . . 1
                (d) AAVS(AVODOD) . . . . . 1

    d. ADC

        (1) HEADQUARTERS
            (a) ADODC . . . . . . . . 1
            (b) ADOOP . . . . . . . . 1
            (c) ADLCC . . . . . . . . 1

        (2) AIR FORCES
            (a) 1AF(DO) . . . . . . . 1
            (b) 10AF
                1. ODC . . . . . . . . 1
                2. PDP-P . . . . . . . 1
            (c) AF ICELAND(FICAS) . . 2

        (3) AIR DIVISIONS
            (a) 25AD(ODC) . . . . . . 2
            (b) 29AD(ODC) . . . . . . 1
            (c) 31AD(CCR) . . . . . . 2
            (d) 33AD(OIN) . . . . . . 1
            (e) 34AD(OIN) . . . . . . 2
            (f) 35AD(CCR) . . . . . . 1
            (g) 37AD(ODC) . . . . . . 1

    e. ATC

        (1) HEADQUARTERS
            (a) ATXDC . . . . . . . . 1

    f. AFLC

        (1) HEADQUARTERS
            (a) MCVSS . . . . . . . . 1
            (b) MCOO . . . . . . . . . 1

    g. AFSC

        (1) HEADQUARTERS
            (a) SCLAP . . . . . . . . 3
            (b) SCS-6 . . . . . . . . 1
            (c) SCGCH . . . . . . . . 2
            (d) SCTPL . . . . . . . . 1
            (e) ASD/ASJT . . . . . . . 1
            (f) ESD/ESO . . . . . . . 1
            (g) RADC/EMOEL . . . . . . 2
            (h) ADTC/ADGT . . . . . . 1

    h. USAFSS

        (1) HEADQUARTERS
            (a) ODC . . . . . . . . . 1
            (b) CHO . . . . . . . . . 1

        (2) SUBORDINATE UNITS
            (a) Eur Scty Rgn(OPD-P) . . 1
            (b) 6940 Scty Wg(OOD) . . . 1

    i. AAC

        (1) HEADQUARTERS
            (a) ALDOC-A . . . . . . . 2

    j. USAFSO

        (1) HEADQUARTERS
            (a) COH . . . . . . . . . 1

    k. PACAF

        (1) HEADQUARTERS

            (a) DP . . . . . . . . . . 1
            (b) DI . . . . . . . . . . 1
            (c) DPL . . . . . . . . . 4
            (d) CSH . . . . . . . . . 1
            (e) DOTEC . . . . . . . . 5
            (f) DE . . . . . . . . . . 1
            (g) DM . . . . . . . . . . 1
            (h) DOTECH . . . . . . . . 1

(2) AIR FORCES
   (a) 5AF(DOPP). . . . . . . 1
      1. Det 8, ASD(DOASD) . 1
   (b) 7AF
      1. DO. . . . . . . . . 1
      2. DIXA. . . . . . . . 1
      3. DPL . . . . . . . . 1
      4. TACC. . . . . . . . 1
      5. DOAC. . . . . . . . 2
   (c) 13AF
      1. CSH . . . . . . . . 1
      2. DPL . . . . . . . . 1
   (d) 7AF/13AF(CHECO). . . . 1

(3) AIR DIVISIONS
   (a) 313AD(DOI) . . . . . . 1
   (b) 314AD(DOP) . . . . . . 2
   (c) 327AD
      1. DO. . . . . . . . . 1
      2. DI. . . . . . . . . 1
   (d) 834AD(DO). . . . . . . 2

(4) WINGS
   (a) 8TFW(DCOA) . . . . . . 1
   (b) 12TFW(DCOI) . . . . . 1
   (c) 35TFW(DCOI) . . . . . 1
   (d) 37TFW(DCOI) . . . . . 1
   (e) 56SOW(DXI) . . . . . . 1
   (f) 347TFW(DCOOT) . . . . 1
   (g) 355TFW(DCOC) . . . . . 1
   (h) 366TFW(DCO) . . . . . 1
   (i) 388TFW(DCO) . . . . . 1
   (j) 405FW(DCOA) . . . . . 1
   (k) 432TRW(DCOI) . . . . . 1
   (l) 460TRW(DCOI) . . . . . 1
   (m) 475TFW(DCO) . . . . . 1
   (n) 633SOW(DCOI) . . . . . 1
   (o) 6400 Test Sq(A). . . . 1

(5) OTHER UNITS
   (a) Task Force Alpha(DXI). 1
   (b) 504TASG(DO). . . . . . 1

m. USAFE
  (1) HEADQUARTERS
    (a) ODC/OA . . . . . . . 1
    (b) ODC/OTA. . . . . . . 1
    (c) OOT . . . . . . . . 1
    (d) XDC . . . . . . . . 1

  (2) AIR FORCES
    (a) 3AF(ODC) . . . . . . 2
    (b) 16AF(ODC). . . . . . 2
    (c) 17AF
      1. ODC . . . . . . . 1
      2. OID . . . . . . . 1

  (3) WINGS
    (a) 20TFW(CACC) . . . . 1
    (b) 36TFW(DCOID) . . . . 1
    (c) 50TFW(DCO) . . . . . 1
    (d) 66TRW(DCOIN-T) . . . 1
    (e) 81TFW(DCO) . . . . . 1
    (f) 401TFW(DCOI) . . . . 1
    (g) 513TAW(OID) . . . . 1
    (h) 7101ABW(DCO-CP) . . 1
    (i) 7149TFW(DCOI) . . . 1

4. SEPARATE OPERATING AGENCIES

a. ACIC(ACOMC) . . . . . . . . 2
b. ARPC(RPCAS-22). . . . . . . 2
c. AFRES(AFRXPL) . . . . . . . 2
d. USAFA
  (1) CMT . . . . . . . . . . 1
  (2) DFH . . . . . . . . . . 1
e. AU
  (1) ACSC-SA. . . . . . . . 1
  (2) AUL(SE)-69-108 . . . . 2
  (3) ASI(ASD-1) . . . . . . 1
  (4) ASI(ASHAF-A) . . . . . 2

# TABLE OF CONTENTS

| | Page |
|---|---|
| FOREWORD | x |
| CHAPTER I - THE AIRLIFT EXPERIENCE IN VIETNAM | 1 |
|     Background of Tactical Airlift Organization | 1 |
|     Tactical Airlift Achievements - Scale and Chronology | 7 |
| CHAPTER II - COMMAND AND CONTROL PROBLEMS | 43 |
| CHAPTER III - MATERIEL PROBLEMS | 83 |
| CHAPTER IV - AERIAL PORT OPERATIONS IN SOUTHEAST ASIA | 106 |
| CHAPTER V - FUTURE ALTERNATIVES | 124 |
| FOOTNOTES | |
|     Foreword | 127 |
|     Chapter I | 127 |
|     Chapter II | 132 |
|     Chapter III | 139 |
|     Chapter IV | 144 |
|     Chapter V | 146 |
| GLOSSARY | 147 |

| FIGURES | Follows Page |
|---|---|
| 1. Airlift Organization, July 1966 | 2 |
| 2. Airlift Organizational Changes, Nov 66 | 4 |
| 3. Airlift Reorganization, Nov 68 | 6 |
| 4. Airlift: Hours Flown, Acft Possessed In-Country, Tonnage Hauled | 8 |
| 5. Republic of Vietnam | 10 |
| 6. Emergency Requests Fulfilled | 28 |
| 7. Tonnage Hauled, Airlift Acft Possessed | 30 |
| 8. Tonnage Hauled Per Flying Hour | 32 |
| 9. Command and Control Organization | 44 |
| 10. C-7A Caribou | 52 |

|   |   | Follows Page |
|---|---|---|
| 11. | Tonnage Hauled - Hours Flown, C-7 | 58 |
| 12. | C-123 Provider | 60 |
| 13. | Tonnage Hauled - Hours Flown, C-123 | 62 |
| 14. | C-130B Hercules Making an ARC LAPES Extraction | 64 |
| 15. | Tonnage Hauled Per Flying Hour, C-130 | 70 |
| 16. | C-130 Statistics | 70 |
| 17. | Artillery Warning System, RVN | 72 |
| 18. | C-7A OR and NORS Status | 92 |
| 19. | C-123 OR and NORS Status | 96 |
| 20. | Organizational Chart, 2d APG (After Nov 66) | 106 |

## FOREWORD

Tactical airlift has been playing an ever-increasing role in the United States' effort in Vietnam, since the first C-123s of the 315th Air Division arrived during January 1962.[1] CHECO report, "Assault Airlift Operations", published on 23 February 1967, reviewed this tactical airlift effort through the last half of 1966.[2] "Tactical Airlift in Vietnam" describes the conduct of tactical airlift operations since that time, discusses some of the problems which have arisen within the system, and sets forth solutions attempted, the extent to which they have succeeded or failed. The tactical airlift organization has been involved in many activities which have had little or nothing to do with airlift in the strictest sense of the word. Such activities include the conduct of flare FAC missions, the dispensing of herbicide on jungle cover or crops, the flying of Airborne Battlefield Command and Control Center missions, the clearing of helipads by means of dropping bombs from C-130s, area denial missions through the dropping of contaminated petroleum in drums from C-130s, and the conduct of psychological warfare operations from C-130s. Since nearly all of these operations have been described in other CHECO reports, only those operations involving the movement of passengers and cargo within Vietnam will be discussed.

CHAPTER I

THE AIRLIFT EXPERIENCE IN VIETNAM

## Background of Tactical Airlift Organization

Tactical airlift is nothing new in Vietnam. Even before Dien Bien Phu in 1954, the United States Air Force was in a small way involved in that endeavor. In those days, 315th Air Division personnel were giving some maintenance and training support to the French C-119 crews which were carrying out the airlift for the forces fighting the Viet Minh. 1/ In its own right, however, the United States Air Force first became involved in airlift in Vietnam when, in January 1962, the 315th Air Division sent some of its own C-123s to Saigon in a temporary duty status. 2/ From that point, the airlift organization in Vietnam has grown to where it is itself an Air Division, the 834th, and where it usually has under its operational control more than two hundred transport aircraft.

Until the last half of 1966, the airlift organization in Vietnam remained a more or less temporary structure (Fig. 1). The whole effort was controlled by the 315th Air Division, then based at Tachikawa Air Base, Japan. The principal subordinate unit in Southeast Asia was the 315th Air Commando Wing, which then had its headquarters at Tan Son Nhut Air Base in Saigon. That Wing was composed of four C-123 squadrons: two located with the Wing headquarters, a third at Nha Trang, and a fourth at Da Nang. 3/ Though the agreement for the transfer had already been made, the C-7s still belonged to the Army during the summer of 1966, and the 2d Aerial Port Group, which had been established at Tachikawa during the preceding spring, supplied the port facilities in Vietnam for the 315th Air Commando Wing.

1

The 315th Air Division also supplied varying numbers of C-130s to the in-country airlift effort and these craft operated out of detachments at Tan Son Nhut, Nha Trang, Tuy Hoa, Cam Ranh Bay and, for a time, even Vung Tau. The Air Force component of the Military Assistance Command, Vietnam, (MACV) in early 1966 was the 2d Air Division, which was headquartered at Tan Son Nhut. The 2d Air Division, and later the Seventh Air Force, exercised operational control over all USAF airlift resources in-country through the 315th Air Commando Wing. These resources included the aforementioned C-130s which came from troop carrier wings based in Okinawa, Taiwan, and the Philippines, as well as Japan.[4/] They were operated in a shuttle system which called for sending the aircraft in-country soon after their phase inspections had been completed and operating them there for ten or twelve days before returning them to their home bases for any heavy maintenance or periodic inspections which were required.

During the summer of 1966, the philosophy was to supply the absolute minimum of maintenance to the C-130 fleet while it was in-country, and this was governed by a rule which demanded that any aircraft which could not be brought into a combat ready status within 24 hours would be returned to its home base in exchange for an operationally ready aircraft. The C-123s, on the other hand, received nearly all of their maintenance in-country and operated under the standard PACAF guideline of maintaining at least 71 percent of the fleet in an operationally ready status at all times.

The requirements for airlift in-country had been growing in a more or less direct proportion to the increase in the commitments of the United States since mid-1964, and it is not surprising that the old organization

# AIRLIFT ORGANIZATION
## JULY 1966

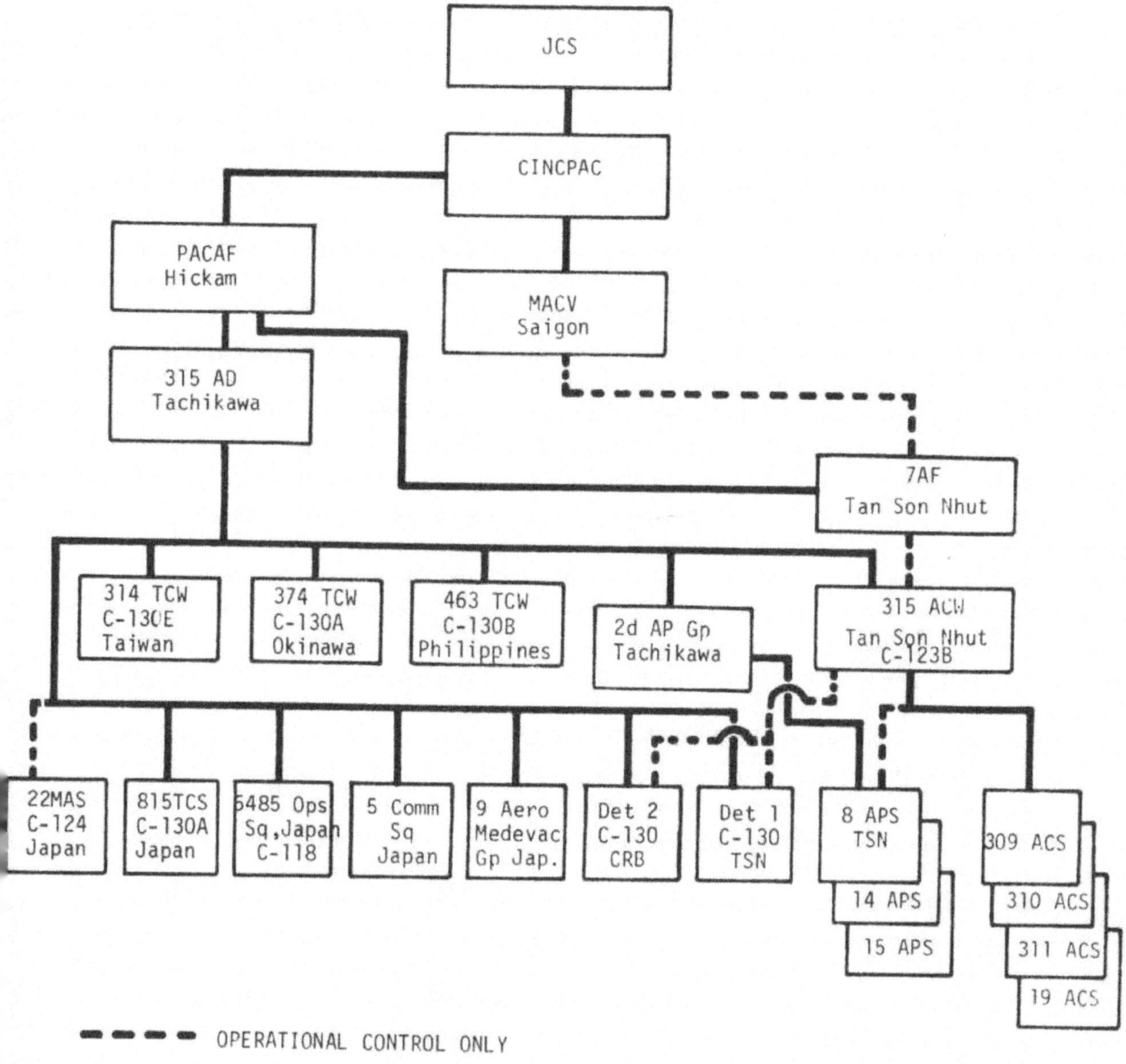

FIGURE I

should have become somewhat inadequate by mid-1966. The Army was complaining that there was insufficient airlift in-country and that the available aircraft was not responsive enough because of inadequate communications.[5/] The Airlift Control Center (ALCC) of the 315th Air Commando Wing did not have a dedicated communications net and often had to depend on long distance telephone to communicate with its subordinate control elements.[6/] The Commander of MACV had, early in 1966, recommended to the Commander-in-Chief Pacific Command (CINCPAC) that an Air Division be established in-country specifically dedicated to the better management of USAF airlift resources.[7/] The 2d Air Division had been deactivated in April 1966, and, in effect, was elevated to Air Force status by the creation of Seventh Air Force out of its resources.[8/] The MACV proposal for an airlift air division was adopted and the 834th was established at Tan Son Nhut Air Base on 15 October 1966 under the command of Brig. Gen. William C. Moore.

This change (Fig. 2) had three very important features. First, the 315th Air Commando Wing became an organic part of the Air Force component of MACV, as opposed to the earlier arrangement in which 7AF merely had operational control of the unit. Second, the aerial port facilities also became a permanent part of 7AF when the 2d Aerial Port Group was moved from Tachikawa to Tan Son Nhut and made a subordinate unit of the 834th Air Division.[9/] Finally, the Chief of Staff of the United States Army and the Chief of Staff of the United States Air Force made an agreement in the spring of 1966, which better defined the roles of both services in regard to the employment of rotary-wing and fixed-wing aircraft. As a part of that agreement, the Air Force was to take over the Army C-7A resources which were then used in six aviation companies deployed at different locations in the Republic of Vietnam.[10/] Although the transfer of the aircraft was not to become effective until the beginning of 1967, the Air Force organization for their employment was established during October 1966. This was to be the 483d Troop Carrier Wing, headquartered at Cam Ranh Bay and first commanded by Col. Paul J. Mascot, USAF.[11/]

At the time, there was a desire on the part of many of the officers involved with in-country airlift operations that the reorganization include the permanent reassigning of a C-130 Wing to the 834th Air Division to be stationed at Cam Ranh Bay.[12/] The chief arguments in favor of this idea had to do with unity of command. General Moore, among others, believed the TDY status of maintenance and aircrew personnel manning the C-130 effort would lead to instability and divided loyalties which would detract from the efficiency of the operation. The arguments against the stationing of such a Wing at Cam Ranh Bay included the difficulties imposed by manpower ceilings on in-country personnel, the fear that additional personnel in-country on permanent change of station (PCS) would have an undesirable impact on the Vietnamese economy, and the fear that the fleet would be more vulnerable to rocket and mortar attacks under the PCS arrangement.[13/] The question reached the highest levels of the Department of Defense and, after a Headquarters, USAF, Operations Analysis Study concluded that the best arrangement for the C-130s was the shuttle operation, the Secretary of Defense made the decision in favor of the offshore basing of the C-130 fleet.[14/] At the time he approved establishment of the 834th Air

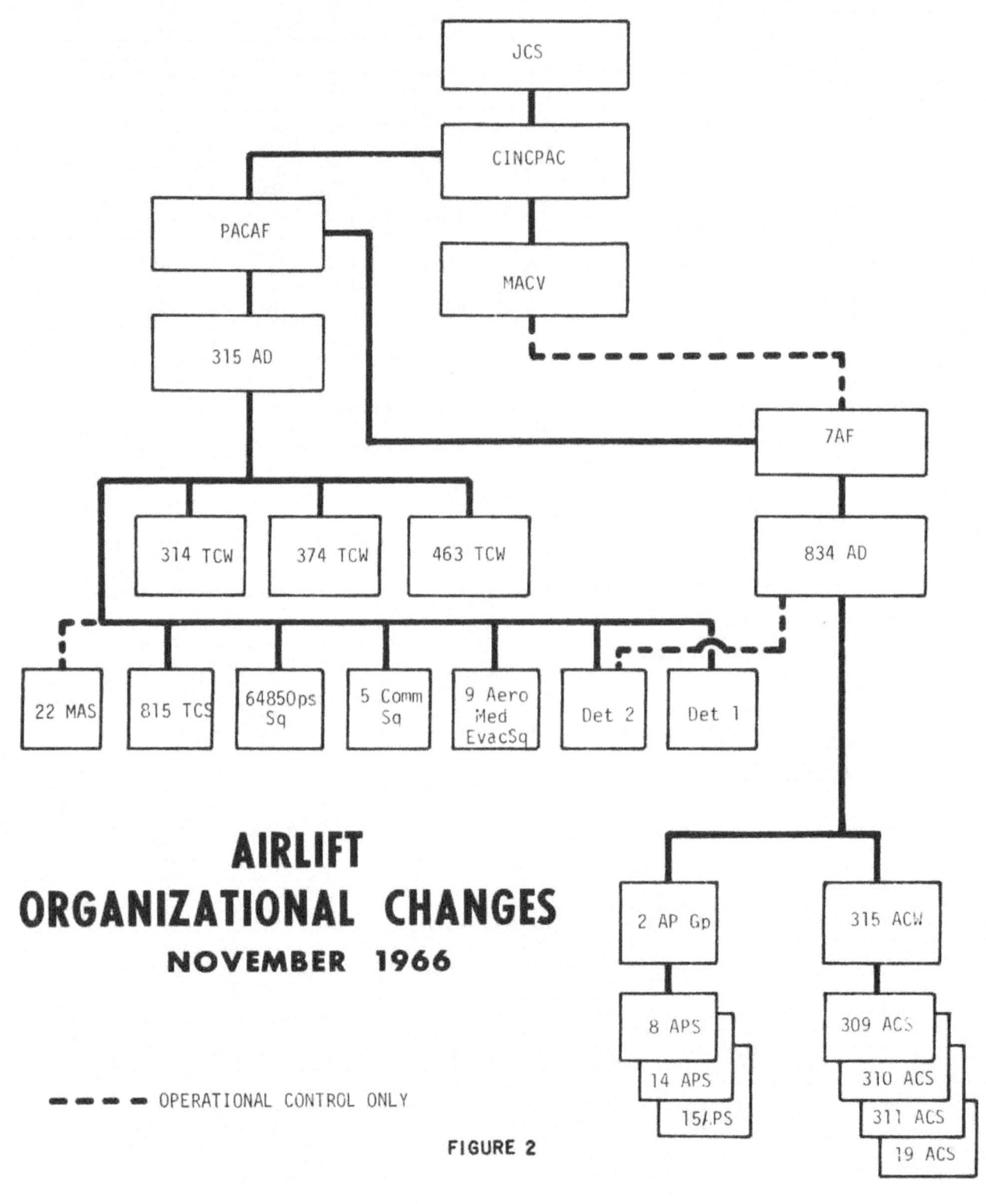

Division, the Chief of Staff of the Air Force had suggested some thought be given to the possibility of eliminating the 315th Air Division and transferring its responsibility for Pacific theater airlift to the Seventh Air Force. 15/

The arguments in favor of deactivation of the 315th Air Division had mainly to do with unity of command. Under the existing arrangement, for example, the 463d Tactical Airlift Wing came under operational control of 7AF for the greater part of its operations, but it came under 13AF for maintenance supervision and various base housekeeping functions; it was under formal command of the 315th Air Division. During the first part of 1967, Headquarters, Pacific Air Forces (PACAF) made a study of the problem and enumerated five possible solutions. In general, these solutions called for the establishment of a Directorate of Airlift at Hickam AFB, Hawaii, for the centralized control of theater airlift. Furthermore, the alternatives called for either reassignment of the remaining responsibilities of the 315th Air Division westward toward Headquarters, 7AF, or eastward toward PACAF. 16/ Placing them under 7AF might have had benefits in terms of better control over the in-country airlift effort. On the other hand, such a move would certainly have been hampered by manpower limitations on the size of the in-country force, as well as by insufficient space and facilities in-country. At the time, the United States had a considerable gold flow problem, and moving the functions of the 315th back to PACAF would have had a favorable impact on that situation. The latter solution, while simplifying the command arrangements, would still have been somewhat defective in terms of unity of command. 17/ The 463d TAW, for example, would have had but one chain of command for all of its Pacific theater functions; however, it would still have been under the operational control of another chain for its in-country work--which remained the most important part of its operations. Finally, since the plan for the post-war period was to return the 834th Air Division to the United States, the arrangement whereby the 315th's functions were to be distributed among PACAF Headquarters and other branches of the PACAF chain of command was clearly superior from the long range point of view.

The Chief of Staff of the Air Force favored eliminating the 315th Air Division and transferring its remaining functions to various units within the PACAF chain of command during May 1968.[18] (Fig. 3). This was, of course, contingent upon the consent of CINCPAC. His approval was given under the conditions that the communications system would prove adequate, and there would be no interruption of airlift within the theater during the move.[19]

The required communications tests were run during the late summer and early fall of 1968, and the reorganization of the PACAF airlift forces became effective during November of that year. The most important changes were: (1) elimination of the 315th Air Division; (2) creation of a Directorate of Airlift at PACAF Headquarters; (3) reassignment of the 9th Aeromedical Evacuation Group* to PACAF Headquarters; (4) elimination of the 5th Communications Squadron, and (5) reassignment of the C-130

---

*The 6485th Operations Squadron, a C-118 unit wholly dedicated to medical evacuation operations, had been transferred from Tachikawa to Clark during January 1968. It was at first made a part of the 463d TAW at its new station, but later was placed directly under the command of the 6th AD.

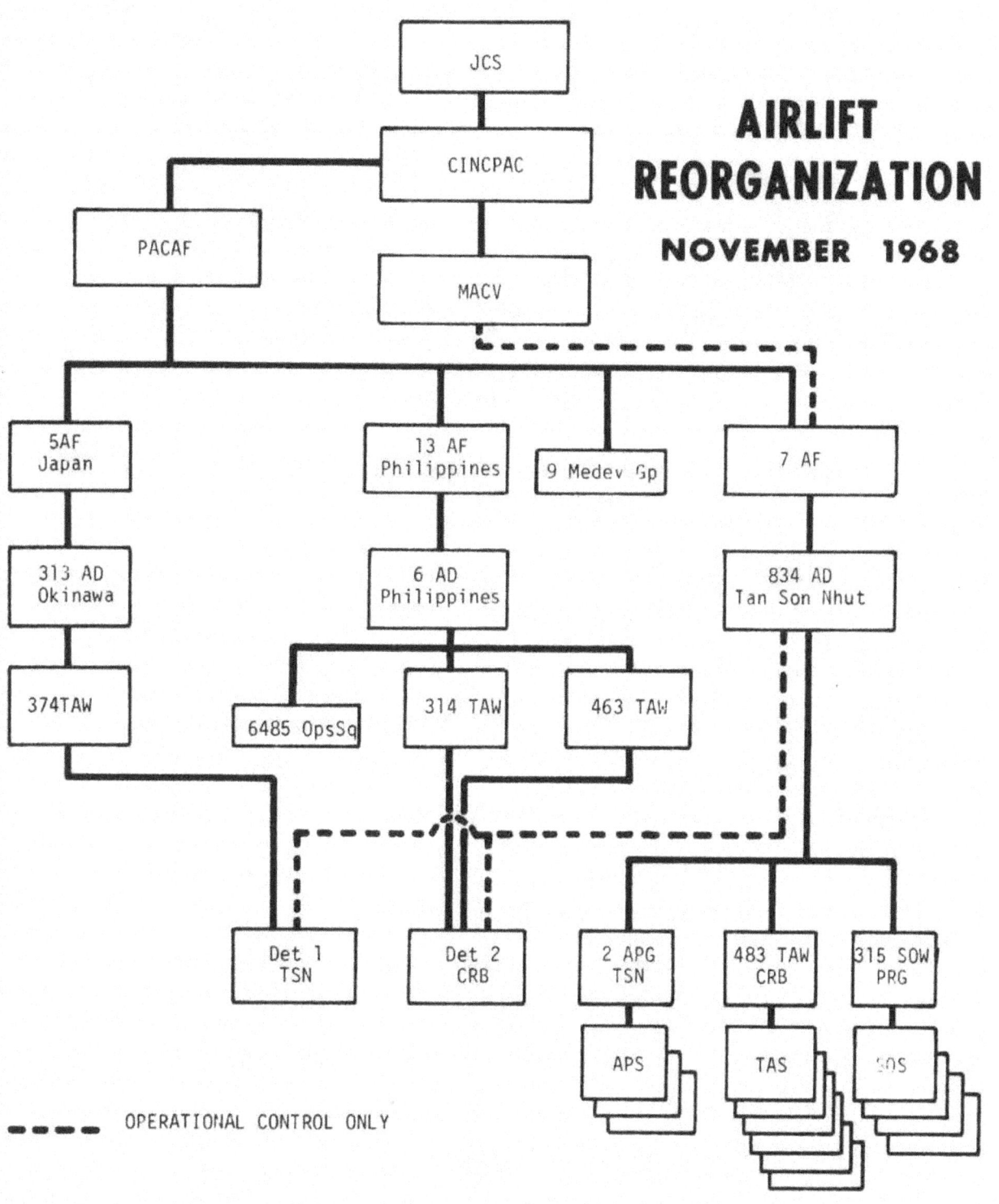

FIGURE 3

tactical airlift wings to 13AF and 5AF.

It is, of course, still too early to evaluate the effects of this latest reorganization. Since it was done partly out of consideration of the post-war organizational needs of PACAF, much depends on the outcome of the current Paris peace talks. The problem of unity of command of the C-130 units remained. Maj. Gen. Burl McLaughlin, Commander of the 834th Air Division, believed, however, that it would be inadvisable to relocate a C-130 unit in-country, at least until the outcome of the peace negotiations.[20/]

In summary, the organizational history of the tactical airlift forces in Southeast Asia began with a series of temporary measures taken to fulfill what were thought to be short-term airlift requirements using the resources of the 315th Air Division. As the war continued beyond its original expectations and airlift requirements grew ever larger, it became apparent that a larger and more permanent organization was needed. Thus, the 834th Air Division was created, again using resources of the 315th Air Division and again eroding the responsibilities of the latter organization. Even at that time, it was becoming apparent, certain inefficiencies were arising due to the fact that the organization for the control of airlift was unduly cumbersome. In an effort to simplify, the 315th Air Division was finally eliminated, and tactical airlift came under the control of two centers--Tan Son Nhut and Hickam--rather than the former three.

Tactical Airlift Achievements - Scale and Chronology

Within the organizational context just described, the achievements of the airlift system follow in a treatment divided into two parts: first, a brief statistical analysis to try to describe the scale of the effort; and second, a choronological narrative which will tell of the flavor of the experience in Vietnam.

During the closing months of 1966, about 95 aircraft under operational control of the 834th Air Division were hauling about 70,000 tons per month. All of this cargo was moved by the C-123s of the 315th Air Commando Wing and the C-130s of the 315th Air Division. A few Vietnamese Air Force (VNAF) C-47s were still under operational control of the 834th, but they were to be released before the end of the year. Approximately six Royal Australian Air Force CV-2s (C-7As) were also under operational control of the 834th Air Division. The Army's CV-2s (Air Force nomenclature: C-7As) were not yet assigned to the Air Force, although Air Force personnel were already attached to the Army Aviation Companies in training for the transition which was to take place early in 1967. The line representing numbers of aircraft in Fig. 4 takes a radical jump in January 1967 and that is due to the addition of six squadrons of 16 C-7s each to the airlift force. The curve representing cargo hauled rises at the same time, but its rate of change is less radical because the load carrying capacity of the C-7 is considerably smaller than that of the C-123 and the C-130. It can also be seen from the same graph that the numbers of aircraft and the cargo hauled were continuously increasing long before the beginning of the Tet Offensive on 31 January 1968, and the 834th Air Division had more than two hundred aircraft under its control for almost two months before that date. The seizure of the Pueblo occurred a few days before Tet and caused the dispatch of some TAC C-130s

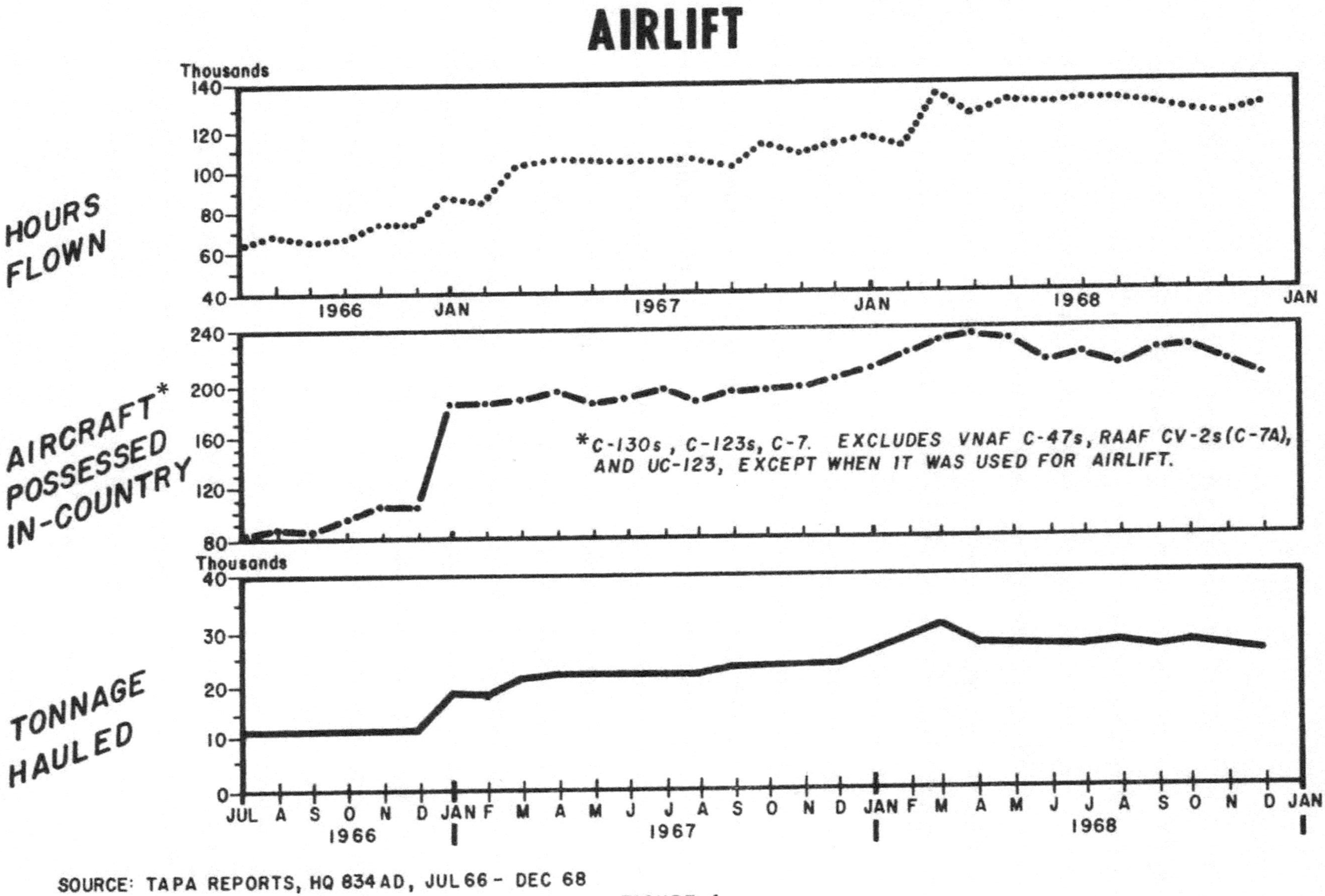
AIRLIFT
HOURS FLOWN
Thousands
140
120
100
80
60
40
1966
JAN
1967
JAN
1968
JAN
AIRCRAFT* POSSESSED IN-COUNTRY
240
200
160
120
80
*C-130s, C-123s, C-7. EXCLUDES VNAF C-47s, RAAF CV-2s (C-7A), AND UC-123, EXCEPT WHEN IT WAS USED FOR AIRLIFT.
TONNAGE HAULED
Thousands
40
30
20
10
0
JUL A S O N D JAN F M A M J J A S O N D JAN F M A M J J A S O N D JAN
1966
1967
1968
SOURCE: TAPA REPORTS, HQ 834 AD, JUL 66 - DEC 68

FIGURE 4

to the Far East and the alerting of others for such a move. Thus, the airlift force had a running start on the buildup when the explosion came. The curve representing numbers of aircraft peaked out during April 1968 at an average of 235.1. This figure also includes some UC-123s of the 12th Special Operations Squadron (SOS) of Bien Hoa Air Base. The weather at the time of Tet was unsuitable for spraying operations, and the airlift requirements were so urgent that these aircraft were converted to the cargo configuration and used in that capacity for several weeks during February and March.[21] As General McLaughlin pointed out:[22] the addition of aircraft or flying time to an airlift system does not necessarily increase the amount of cargo moved. It sometimes results in a decrease in efficiency because of the saturation of facilities such as that which occured in February 1968, when the amount of cargo hauled declined (Fig. 4), although flying time and numbers of aircraft increased. The reverse was true in June 1968, however, when the numbers of aircraft and hours flown both declined without a corresponding decline in the amount of cargo hauled. Though the numbers of aircraft peaked in April, the maximum cargo (136,745 tons) was hauled in March. The peak in flying hours came in the same month when 31,436 hours were logged by an average number of 232.6 aircraft.[23]

Operation EL PASO was already underway during July 1966 in the troublesome area between Saigon and the Cambodian border (Fig. 5) to the north. Free World Forces won all five of their engagements with the enemy during the operation and in three of them tactical airpower was the decisive factor.[24] The air line of communications was the only line of communications for many of the troops on several occasions. During the course of the campaign, C-130s and C-123s flew 6,650 sorties to move more than 30,000 troops and 19,000 tons of cargo. [25]

Operation ATTLEBORO, a successor to EL PASO in the same area, took place during the fall of 1966, it required another massive airlift operation. The C-130s and C-123s flew 3,314 sorties and airlanded 10,270 tons of cargo and passengers in direct support of the Army forces in contact with the enemy. In the words of the historian of the operation: [26]

> *"While American forces were busy overrunning the enemy stronghold, a fantastic quantity of men, ammunition, artillery and supplies were being poured into the battle area from all over the southern half of Vietnam, in what was to be the largest tactical emergency airlift operation of the war. Twin-engined C-123s and giant four-engined C-130s were landing continuously at Tay Ninh and the forward base airstrips. This tremendous effort was, for the most part, responsible for the buildup of American Forces in such a short time. Once the enemy committed himself to battle, the entire area came under a virtual deluge of men and equipment, brought in by airlift. The value of quick deployment of forces was amply demonstrated during the crucial battles of the previous few days."*

While Operation ATTLEBORO was going on in the south, two struggles were taking place farther north: one at each end of the vital Route 19, which bisects South Vietnam as it runs from Qui Nhon on the coast to Pleiku in the central highlands. Operation PAUL REVERE and its successor, Operation SAM HOUSTON, were battles which took place at the western end of the artery, while the fighting around Qui Nhon and Phu Cat in the east were referred to as Operation THAYER I, Operation IRVING, and Operation THAYER II.

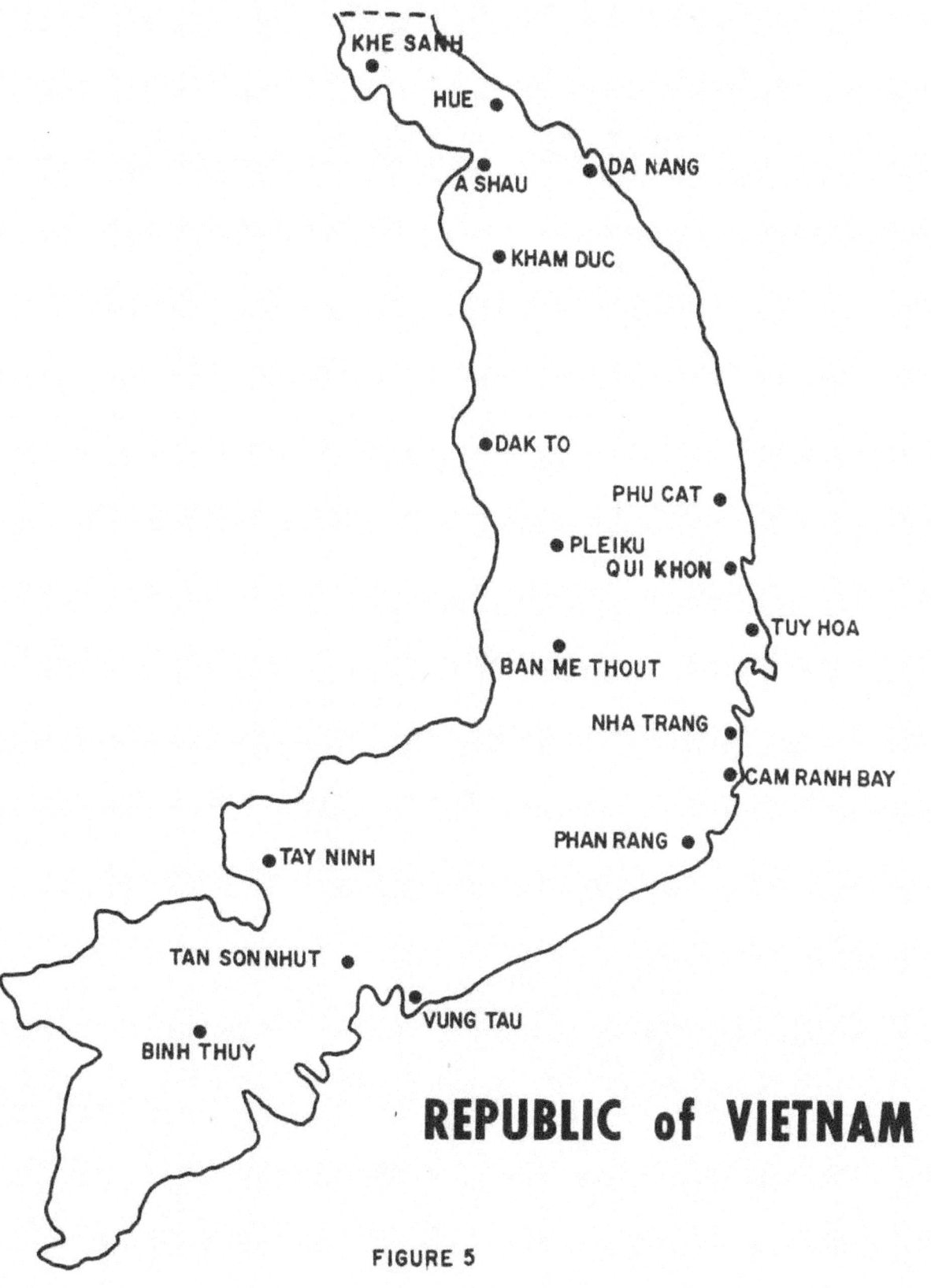

**REPUBLIC of VIETNAM**

FIGURE 5

UNCLASSIFIED

The enemy's plan for the latter part of 1966 in the Pleiku area was to make thrusts across the border from his sanctuary in Cambodia against the special forces camps to the west and north of Pleiku in the hope of overrunning them, and ultimately moving down Highway 19 to the sea and cutting South Vietnam in two, thereby isolating the northern part of the country.[27/] The goals of Operations PAUL REVERE and SAM HOUSTON included the defense of the supply route on the coast, the defense and pacification of the area around Pleiku, and the breaking of the enemy's will to continue the fight.

During the fall of 1966, in Operation PAUL REVERE, the enemy ran into a string of reverses when he attempted to attack the Free World Forces in prepared positions where it was easier for them to request close air support. He learned his lesson, however, and after the first of the year, he shifted his tactics to making attacks on the Allied forces when they were on the move and out of their fortifications, where it would be more difficult to use tactical airpower. Both PAUL REVERE and SAM HOUSTON were nevertheless successful from the Allied point of view,[28/] and a part of their success was due to the effectiveness of tactical airlift as well as close air support.

During PAUL REVERE, for example, fifty C-123 sorties were expended in making drops of critically needed artillery ammunition at isolated places. Out of the 6,100 rounds of 105-mm, 155-mm, and 175-mm ammunition which were dropped, only 166 were lost because of bad drops or parachute malfunctions. The Army considered these drops so responsive to their needs, they planned to increase the use of them in future operations.[29/]

Airland operations were equally important to the success of the Free World Forces. As expressed in Project CHECO Report "Operation PAUL REVERE/SAM HOUSTON":

> "USAF Operations were absolutely essential to the success of PAUL REVERE II. Between 1-4 August, a tactical emergency airlift transported the 1/7th Cav Task Force, the 3d Fire Support Element, and supporting artillery from Dak To to LZ (Landing Zone) Oasis with 32 C-130, 7 C-123, and 18 Army CV-2E (C-7A) sorties. Between 1845 hours on 2 August and 1440 hours on 3 August, a total of 39 C-130 sorties moved the 2d Bde Task Force from An Khe to Pleiku. Again on 15 August, 16 C-130 sorties assisted in the movement of several units in conjunction with the operation. Supply became an extremely critical factor in maintaining the troops and equipment in the field when Highway 19, between LZ Oasis and Duc Co SF (Special Forces) Camp, became impassable to wheeled vehicles because of adverse weather conditions and tank traffic on the road."

At that time, an Air Line of Communications (ALOC) then set up to overcome that difficulty.[30/] SAM HOUSTON was the new name given to PAUL REVERE with the coming of 1967 and tactical airlift support helped again from 19-21 February 1967 when 75 C-130 sorties were committed to move the 1st Brigade of the 4th Infantry Division from Tuy Hoa to Pleiku.[31/]

Meanwhile at the other end of Highway 19, Operations THAYER and IRVING were also administering a string of reverses to the enemy. The purposes of the Allied forces were to secure the eastern end of the highway, to pacify the area around Qui Nhon and Phu Cat, and to prevent the infiltration of the area by sea. The enemy was dealt a considerable defeat--more than 4,000 were confirmed dead and its VC units had suffered a great degeneration in morale by the end of the period--many of its troops were deserting and going back to their villages.[32/]

Neither close air support nor tactical airlift played as important a role in this operation as they had in PAUL REVERE and SAM HOUSTON. The Koreans involved were hesitant about using close air support because they had not been oriented in their training for this type of support. Moreover, they proved reluctant to wait for the 20 minutes or more, required after the initial contact to bring in air support to soften up their targets. They would rather immediately engage the enemy with only artillery support and were usually too closely engaged to permit the commitment of air when the aircraft arrived on the scene.33/

Only 349 C-130 and C-123 sorties were flown in support of the operations. They moved more than a thousand tons of cargo and four thousand passengers into the battle zone.34/ Tactical airlift was less important to THAYER-IRVING than it had been to the operations in the Pleiku area, partly because the battle zone was quite handy to a major supply point served by the sea lift forces (Qui Nhon), and also because the 1st Air Cavalry had large helicopter resources which were extensively used for resupply during the campaign.

Operation JUNCTION CITY started just as Operations THAYER II and SAM HOUSTON were coming to an end; it was the first big U.S. airborne effort of the war. It was scheduled to begin at 0700 hours on 22 February 1967. The airborne part of the operation was planned to drop troops north of Tay Ninh, just south of the Cambodian border, and across the escape routes into Cambodia. Other Allied forces were then to drive up from the south and, it was hoped, to thus trap the enemy forces fleeing for the safety of the Cambodian sanctuary. Eight hundred forty-five troops, along with 20 airplane loads of supplies, were successfully dropped, and another 2,057 airlift sorties carried 17,524 passengers and 11,307 tons of cargo to the forward fields in direct support of the Allied forces involved in the battle.[35/]

The summer of 1967 was passed in more or less routine operations on an ever-increasing scale for the airlift forces. During November 1967, the battle of Dak To took place. The American forces were sitting astride a good route into South Vietnam in the central highlands and had been expecting an attack for some time. When it occurred, the U.S. ground forces were able to use tactical air with excellent results. The communists suffered a considerable reverse--they did not achieve their objective, and they lost more than 1,600 of their men compared with 344 Allied deaths. They did, however, achieve the destruction of two C-130s engaged in a resupply mission for the U.S. Army and the Army of Republic of Vietnam (ARVN), which were parked at the airfield. The enemy unleashed a very accurate mortar attack which immediately destroyed two of the aircraft. A third was saved by the pilot and the engineer who, right in the middle of the attack, moved it away from the other burning C-130s to prevent its loss, and then flew it back to the home base in spite of the large amount of battle damage their Hercules had suffered. For their part in the action, Capt. Joseph Glenn and Sgt. Joseph Mack were awarded Silver Stars. The field was then closed for a couple of days, but the resupply of forces was resumed 17 November, with only one C-130 allowed on the ground at a time.[36/]

As can be seen from the tonnage curve in Figure 4, the work load for tactical airlift forces remained fairly stable during the first half of

1967. During the latter half of the year, rising force levels and special operations led to increasing airlift requirements. For example, during mid-November, the Military Airlift Command (MAC) moved the greater part of the 101st Airborne Division (except one brigade already in Vietnam) directly from Fort Campbell, Kentucky, to Bien Hoa Air Base, Vietnam. This move involved 413 C-133 and C-141 sorties, all of which offloaded at Bien Hoa and Tan Son Nhut. This imposed a tremendous additional load on the 8th Aerial Port Squadron, and then on the entire tactical airlift system as the new troops were absorbed into the force. 37/

These increasing requirements generated the need for increased numbers of aircraft, and as the 834th entered the new year, for the first time in the Vietnamese war, it had under its operational control more than 200 transport planes. Then, on 22 January 1968, the Pueblo was seized by the North Koreans, which caused the dispatch of additional C-130s from the Tactical Air Command (TAC) to PACAF. At the same time, additional TAC C-130 units were alerted for possible service in the Far East. 38/ Thus, though the airlift forces had a running start in terms of numbers of aircraft available when the siege of Khe Sanh and the Tet Offensive began, the facilities for handling this airlift fleet were already nearing satuation. 39/

Although the Tet Offensive and the siege of Khe Sanh occurred simultaneously, the latter will be treated separately because it constitutes a classic example of the use of tactical airlift in its resupply role in a limited war. Though western journalists were pointing out many differences between Khe Sanh and Dien Bien Phu, certain geographical similarities and the political goals of the NVN Defense Minister, General Vo Nguyen Giap's campaign against the Marine base might well have been similar to those he had pursued against the French. The fall of Khe Sanh would certainly have amplified the shock administered to U.S. public opinion as a result of the Tet Offensive and would have made the Administration's problems still more difficult than they were. The purpose of the United States in occupying the base at Khe Sanh was to impede the flow of men and materiel from North Vietnam southward by placing a force astride a major enemy line of communications.

Khe Sanh is situated in a mountain valley less than one hundred miles northwest of Da Nang. There is a small, unnavigable stream which flows down the valley and passes within a few hundred yards of the east end of the runway. This runway is 3,900 feet long and 1,608 feet above sea level. The approach to the base is made by flying up the valley in a westerly direction toward the east-west runway which was made of aluminum matting. There is mountainous terrain in all directions, but the highest ridges are to the north of the valley. The ground rises more abruptly to the west of the field than it does to the south.

The area used as a drop zone was a few hundred yards beyond the western end, and very slightly north of an extended center line of the runway. The weather was quite often bad in that area during February and March. Low ceilings, reduced visibility, and rain were often experienced by the airlift forces supplying Khe Sanh.

The garrison at the Marine base consisted of about 5,000 Marines, about 1,000 ARVN troops, and a few Air Force support personnel. The 834th Air Division maintained a mission commander, a combat control team, and a mobility team at the airfield throughout the siege. 40/ The position was surrounded and brought under siege during the latter part of January 1968.

The decision was made to defend Khe Sanh, and to be sure an extended period of "below-minimums" weather would not prevent resupply of the garrison, a 20-day supply of all essential items was to be maintained. Since airlanding is less expensive than airdropping this tactic was employed for the first few weeks of the siege. C-130s, C-123s, and C-7s were employed at first, but the mortar and small arms fire proved so intense, it was decided to discontinue use of the C-7s. The C-123s could deliver approximately twice the amount of cargo at the same risk--perhaps even less, because of the increased climb rate and greater reliability given to the C-123K by its newly-installed jet engines. 41/ As the operation continued, the combat control team soon realized when an aircraft called that it was inbound, the runway and ramp area could come under mortar fire. Even if this fire did not hit the aircraft, the resulting shrapnel and debris could cut tires and incapacitation due to a flat tire would have left the airplane in an extremely vulnerable position. Though the Marine Commander was reluctant to accept the airdrop method, Gen. William W. Momyer, the 7AF Commander, prohibited further C-130 landings at Khe Sanh on 12 February 1968, right after a Marine C-130 had been destroyed by mortar fire. The

Marines feared the morale of their men might go down if there was a noticeable decline in the number of landings. The Air Force argued, however, that the contrary might be true, since the Marines had surely noticed enemy barrage greatly increased in intensity each time a transport plane touched down--so much so that the aircraft came to be known as "mortar magnets".[42/]

The airdrop phase of the resupply campaign was conducted using three methods: The Container Delivery System (CDS); the Low Altitude Parachute Extraction System (LAPES); and the Ground Proximity Extraction System (GPES). Using the CDS system, the aircraft made a conventional approach to the Drop Zone (DZ) from an initial point several miles away but lined up with the center line of the zone. In the case of the C-130, the airplane crossed the DZ at a speed of 130 knots and an altitude of 600 feet. At the appropriate time, a gate holding the load in the aircraft was cut, and the sixteen 2,000-pound bundles were extracted from the cargo compartment by the force of gravity. The advantages of this sytem were that a large load (in terms of total weight) could be delivered in one pass, and the system had more accuracy than those which required a higher drop altitude. The disadvantages were that any cargo too large or too heavy to fit into one of the standard bundles could not be delivered in this fashion. The delivery technique also required that the aircraft stay at an altitude well within range of small arms for an extended period at a very low speed.

In the LAPES, the cargo was loaded onto a large sled which was extracted from the aircraft by means of a parachute at an altitude between five-to-ten feet. With this system, no particular pattern was required in getting to the extraction zone (EZ), which made it easier to foil enemy gunners. Bulky, heavy items could be delivered, if the total weight did not exceed 18,000 pounds on one pass. (New modifications to the LAPES overcame this limitation and are discussed in Chapter II.) Disadvantages of this system included descending into the zone of vulnerability to ground fire, and the danger to troops and installations when it was used in congested areas. LAPES was completely self-contained; deliveries could be made to relatively flat areas without personnel required to prepare the EZ.

The Ground Proximity Extraction System was not self-contained. It was similar to the LAPES in most respects, but the load was extracted from the airplane by trailing a hook which caught a cable installed by a ground crew. The GPES load was attached either to the aircraft or to the cable on the ground at all times, and it was therefore safer to use in congested areas than was LAPES.[43/] The cargo platforms it used were more abundant and cheaper than LAPES sleds. It delivered the load to the same place every time and therefore eased the recovery problem of the ground troops. Successive loads, however, could not be delivered into the EZ at a pace as rapid as LAPES, because of the necessity of rerigging the arresting cable after each extraction. This system also required that the aircraft descend into the zone of small arms fire.[44/]

Beginning on 13 February 1968, all C-130 deliveries were made by airdrop method, and many C-123 deliveries were made that way, too. The C-123s developed new tactics which proved quite successful. They delayed their descent to the drop altitude until the very last second and then made a maximum performance descent at about 3,000 feet per minute and leveled out at 800 feet, just 12 seconds away from the DZ. Upon reaching the computed air release point (CARP), they dropped the load, then climbed out as rapidly as possible with both their reciprocating and jet engines set at the highest permissible power setting.[45] It was necessary, however, to continue some C-123 airlandings throughout the siege to deliver cargo unfeasible to drop, and bring out wounded personnel.

The LAPES and CDS were used exclusively by the C-130s throughout most of the campaign, but toward the end, the LAPES components were in short supply. It was necessary to bring in GPES equipment from the United States, and quickly train crews in its use (a simple matter since LAPES and GPES procedures were similar). The GPES was then used for the balance of deliveries involving supplies beyond the size and weight limitations of the CDS.[46]

The siege lasted 78 days. During that time, 12,430 tons were delivered to the garrison at Khe Sanh, of which, 4,310 tons were airlanded and the remaining 8,120 tons were dropped. The C-130s made 237 landings, 52 LAPES extractions, 15 GPES extractions, and 496 CDS drops. The C-123s made 179 landings and 105 CDS drops. The circular error average (CEA) for the C-123 drops was 70 yards. The CEA for C-130 drops under Visual Meteorological Conditions (VMC) was 95 yards, and under Instrument Meteorological Conditions (IMC), it was reported to be 133 yards.[47]

Frequent bad weather conditions and heavy enemy fire demanded development of a method to drop supplies under IMC. After considering

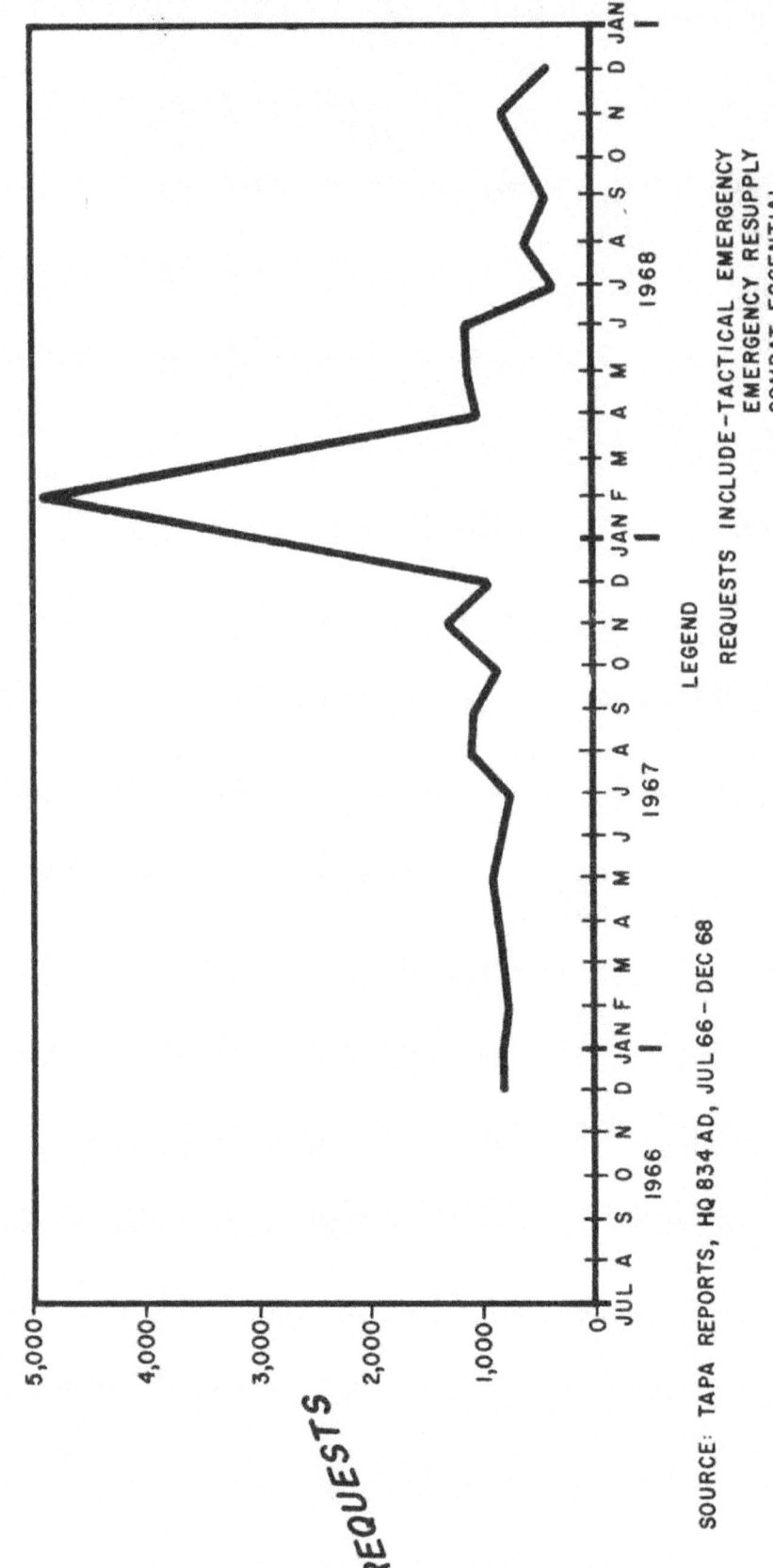

FIGURE 6

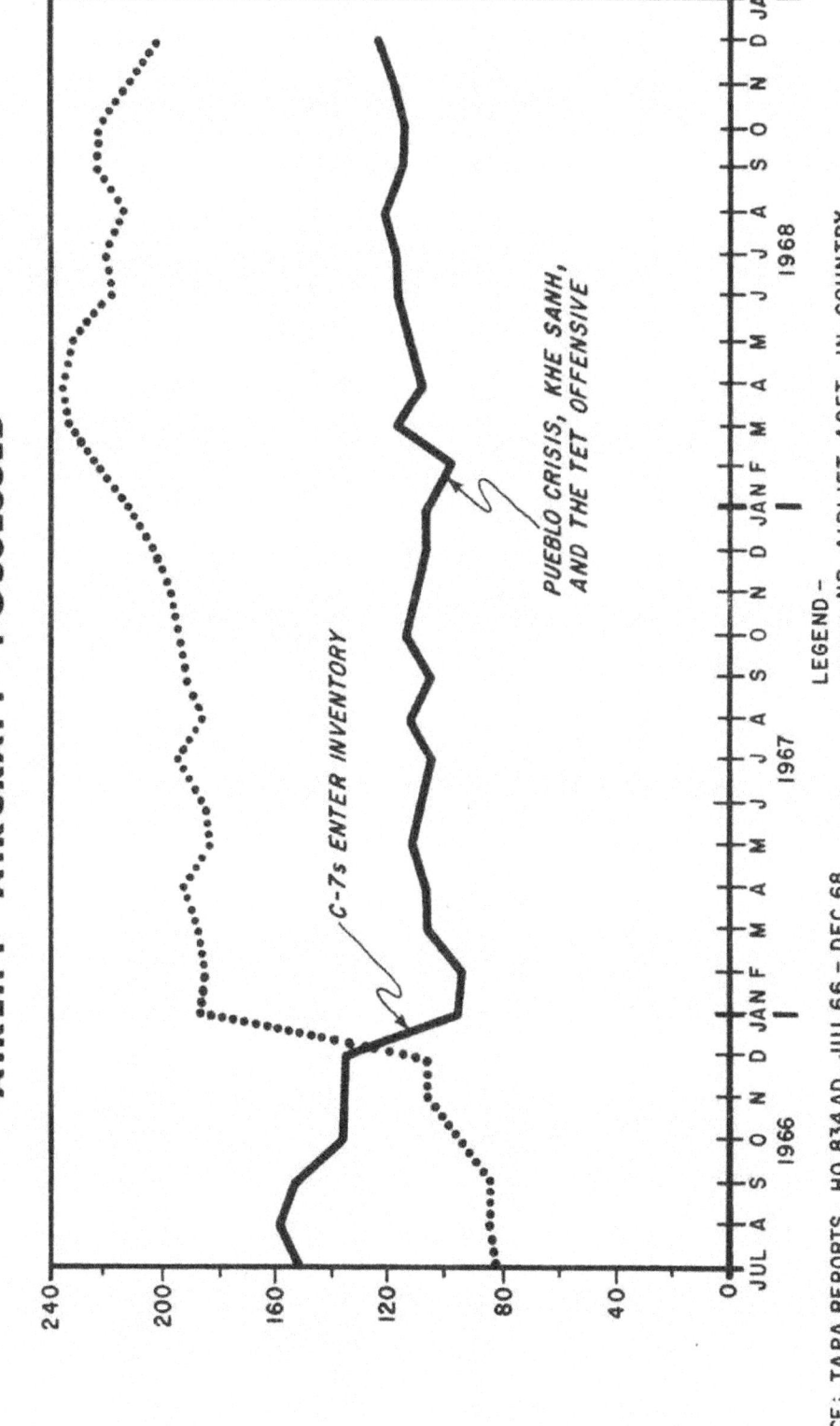

FIGURE 7

numerous alternatives, the 834th Air Division developed an expedient technique which was employed with tremendous success. The technique, a "first" in tactical airlift history, utilized the Ground Controlled Approach (GCA) radar to vector the aircraft over a predetermined geographical point on the ground at low altitude; at that point the aircrew took over. Using known winds in the Doppler navigation system and precise timing techniques, the aircrew would fly to a Computed Air Release Point (CARP) and execute a CDS delivery at the precise elapsed time. Loads were released onto a 300-by-300-yard drop zone (seven hundred yards shorter than standard for a CDS delivery).

When the GCA was knocked out by enemy fire or was down for maintenance, the Khe Sanh TPQ-10 (used primarily for fighter strikes), was successfully used in lieu of the GCA to vector aircraft over a specific point. The significance of these all-weather procedures was borne out in the final analysis which revealed that of the 496 C-130 CDS sorties, 38 percent or 188 deliveries were performed using the IMC procedures. The CEA for these IMC drops was 133 yards. The crews preferred dropping from instrument conditions, because the low clouds reduced the possibility of being hit by enemy ground fire. This IMC technique may prove useful in future operations, where the DZ is conveniently located near a suitable radar installation.

The resupply of Khe Sanh was not without cost. Five transport aircraft were lost: three C-123s (one of them with the entire crew and a full load of passengers), and two C-130s (one Marine Corps aircraft hit by mortar fire and the other, an Air Force plane, which left the runway on landing). Fifty-three aircraft were hit by ground fire and 18 of these were seriously damaged, but they were all reparable.[48/] Very few of the crew members on these damaged aircraft were wounded and none was killed.

Maj. Gen. Burl McLaughlin, Commander of the 834th Air Division, in his *Air University Review* article on Khe Sanh speaks of several lessons which should be drawn from the Khe Sanh experience.[49/] He believed the ultimate in an airdrop system would be a completely self-contained Instrument Meteorological Condition (IMC) capability which would permit precision drops from within or above clouds without any aid from the ground. He also believed a self-contained precision approach aid for airland missions should be developed. According to his article, the USAF should strive for a V/STOL capability which would help in avoiding ground fire, improve the "med-evac" capability, and enable crews to place the load wherever it is required on the base, thus saving lives and money which might be spent in recovery operations. Meanwhile, the USAF should acquire a new, simple Light Intratheater Transport (LIT) with the capability of using fields less than a thousand feet long. Such an aircraft would save the ground forces the tremendous expense of building an approximately 3,000 foot runway required for the C-130. The shorter runway would also be easier to defend. General McLaughlin emphasized that it was very important to design follow-on aircraft with bullet proof tires and with explosion-resistant fuel tanks. He commented that the present fleet should also be equipped with those items. The 834th Commander also pointed out that the layout of a base should include space for a DZ.

Finally, he concluded that experience has demonstrated the need for fighter cover whenever drops are being conducted in a non permissive environment.[50/]

By what criteria would one evaluate the effectiveness of an airlift operation such as Khe Sanh? Ton-mile computations or even tonnage delivered per day are really inappropriate. In fact, they are not even demanded by Air Force doctrine, which explicitly states that responsiveness must always come first in tactical airlift. Thus, though the battle cost five airlift airplanes, one crew, and the lives of one full load of C-123 passengers, there can be no doubt that the garrison was sustained and that General Giap was denied his military and political goals partly because of the airlift operation. It is fair, therefore, to say that the resupply of Khe Sanh was a substantial success for participating airlift forces.

If the airlift system approached an ideal performance in the Khe Sanh resupply campaign, it was at the same time receiving its most severe test in response to the Tet offensive. At the very time a considerable part of its resources was being devoted to the Khe Sanh operation, the ferocity and extent of the offensive stretched the airlift organization almost to the breaking point. It is true that the system held but not without such extraordinary measures as bringing in three C-130 squadrons from the United States, importing more than 300 people from other areas to help man the aerial port system, converting the herbicide fleet to the cargo configuration and, finally, not without extraordinary efforts on the parts of many, many people.

As was pointed out here, the facilities of the tactical airlift system were already near saturation on the eve of Tet. On 12 January 1968, the J-45 section of MACV had written a letter to Seventh Air Force stating the command was approaching a saturation point of C-130 facilities, and suggesting a plan be developed which would allow for a 15-to-20 percent surge capability.51/ The personnel situation might have been worse than that of the facilities had not someone, on the basis of intelligence reports, made the timely decision to bring all C-130B crew members to the Tan Son Nhut Air Base from their downtown hotel. Unfortunately, the C-123 unit at Saigon did not do the same and their aircrews were trapped for several days.

The Allied forces were fortunate that additional airlift airplanes were already inbound to the theater when the offensive started, and that quite by accident, the new Airlift Control Center facility had been occupied just five days earlier. Without these airplanes and the improved control facility, response to the crisis would have been immeasurably more difficult.52/

During the night of 31 January 1968, the Viet Cong and North Vietnamese forces in South Vietnam mounted a massive attack with rocket fire, mortar fire, terrorist activities, and ground assaults against nearly all of the major population centers and Allied bases in the country. The forces of the United States and the Allies were in a particularly exposed position for this kind of attack, for they were heavily committed to operations in the remote areas near the western border of South Vietnam and to pacification programs in the rural areas of the country. This situation generated the need to move large numbers of troops back to the urban areas at the very time when many land lines of communication had been cut by the enemy. The job could be done only by tactical airlift. Moreover, the hauling of troops did not utilize the full weight-carrying capacity of the C-130. At the same time, there were a great many emergency missions to be flown to forward fields with light loads and no return loads. The evacuation of some of the airlift bases was necessary on repeated occasions and this, too, expended sorties that would otherwise have been used to halt the rise in the level of backlogged cargo in the aerial ports.

Tan Son Nhut Air Base was especially vital to the airlift system. The headquarters and command post of the system were located there. Roughly one-third of the C-130 force was then based there. Tan Son Nhut was the "beddown" base for one fourth of the C-123 airplanes. The largest aerial port in the world was also located there. The attack on Tan Son Nhut was, therefore, an especially important part of the strain placed on the tactical airlift organization.

As pointed out earlier, the C-130 crews based at Tan Son Nhut had been recalled from their off-base quarters, but the C-123 crews were trapped in their downtown billets for three days. 53/ Off duty crew members and staff members from Phan Rang were brought to Tan Son Nhut; they flew the idle C-123s back to Phan Rang, where they were operated by crews from the other squadrons, until their own crew members were able to get to the base.

On that first night, the attack on the perimeter at Tan Son Nhut was so threatening, it was the cause of a Tactical Emergency Request. This was fulfilled in a matter of three hours by dispatching C-130s from Saigon to bring in a battalion of South Vietnamese Marines, while the field was under fire. These troops played a vital role in preventing a breach in the perimeter which might well have proved disastrous.[54/] The Air Base also came under rocket and mortar attack from the beginning, and it was necessary to evacuate the airlift force then and on repeated occasions during the ensuing weeks. The C-130s were moved to Phan Rang and Cam Ranh Bay, and this separation from their source of cargo and maintenance further strained the system. Thus, while the ground attacks and rocket fire were not especially damaging in the number of aircraft destroyed, they did impose a considerable loss of cargo-moving capacity because of the great waste involved in evacuation and emergency missions.

The immediate effect of the Offensive was that it caused a tremendous rise in the number of emergency requests. For example, on the very night that the Offensive started, a critical situation developed at Ban Me Thuot. The Allied forces were rapidly running out of ammunition and the 315th Special Operations Wing (SOW) was called upon to bring it in to them on a Tactical Emergency Priority. There were no runway lights and the landings were made under fire by the light of oil fires set in drums placed next to the runway. Though a considerable amount of battle damage was suffered by the C-123s involved, the goods were delivered and no airplanes or crew members were lost.[55/] Two nights later, the U.S. garrison at Kontum found itself in dire straits, and the 315th SOW was again called upon to take in the necessary supplies. Landing at Kontum was impossible, so the first night drops of the war were undertaken. The ground commander radioed that the enemy was attacking the perimeter, and the entire base would have to be used for a drop zone. He placed a light on the top of his command bunker as a target; again the goods were delivered, and they helped to save the camp from being overrun.[56/]

As dramatic as these emergency missions were, they nevertheless added a further strain on the airlift system. In the first place, very seldom did any cargo have to be hauled back from the forward location, so at least 50 percent of the effort represented unused cargo hauling capacity. Then, too, this situation grew worse--the important thing about an emergency cargo is the intensity of its need and the timeliness of its delivery--not its size. It can become necessary to employ a C-130 to deliver 25 pounds of blood to some forward base, regardless of whether the remaining 35,000 pounds of its cargo-carrying capacity can be utilized. The unusual number of emergency requests which arose from the Offensive thus consumed an extraordinary amount of airlift capability at a critical time.

All of these factors added to the saturation of the system and, insofar as the priority plan was concerned, tended to place the airlift managers in a dilemma which became worse as the Offensive continued. MACV uses a priority system comprised of three emergency categories, deemed sufficiently important to disrupt the scheduled airlift missions, and four lesser, routine priorities. Beginning with the most important category, they are labelled: Tactical Emergency (TE requires the requestor to be in contact with the enemy or that contact be imminent); Emergency Resupply (ER); Combat Essential (CE); and thence priorities 1 through 4. Priority 2, 3, or 4 cargo seldom moves by air. Urgent medical evacuation missions are considered to have the same priority as Tactical Emergency. The graph in Figure 6 shows the number of emergency requests fulfilled in January 1968 (2891) was triple what it had been during the previous month (942). The initial impact of the Tet Offensive caused the surge in emergency requests, which in turn brought about a kind of "domino effect" in the entire priority system. The initial surge caused the cancellation of a great number of scheduled and preplanned airlift missions. This cancellation caused the delay of cargo waiting for transportation with routine priorities, which, in turn, impaired the supply situation at many forward locations.

Accordingly, the commanders raised the priorities of their requests, which generated more emergency missions. This situation also caused more routine missions to be cancelled; then more emergency requests were generated, until the greater part of the missions flown were of the emergency categories.[57] By February 1968, the system was so inundated, that some Combat Essential (CE) requests could not be serviced.[58] It was possible, however, to meet all the requirements for Tactical Emergency and Emergency Resupply missions throughout the offensive. The number of emergency requests continued to rise at a radical rate, until they reached a figure of 4,939 in February.[59]

The steps taken to bring about a recovery from the initial shock that the Tet Offensive administered to the airlift system included the addition of aircraft, increasing personnel; providing arbitrary moves to end the escalation of emergency requests; and restoring scheduled and preplanned service to the airlift effort.

As was mentioned earlier, one TAC C-130 squadron had already been ordered to proceed to the Far East. Another, which had been placed on alert for a similar move prior to the outbreak of the offensive was ordered to Japan early in February.[60/] These two organizations were based at Tachikawa and placed under operational control of the 315th Air Division. A third C-130 squadron was sent to Clark Air Base in the Philippines to augment MAC, but it, too, was placed under the operational control of the 315th soon after its arrival.[61/] These moves made it possible for the 315th to fulfill the airlift requirements arising from the Pueblo crisis, and at the same time raise the level of its in-country C-130 force. The peak figure was 96 aircraft in March, but the averages were 89.0 for February, 90.5 for March, and 92.7 for April.[62/] Additional airlift capacity was found in the 12th Special Operations Squadron at Bien Hoa. The mission of the 12th was defoliation, but the weather at the time of Tet greatly hampered the conduct of that operation. The aircraft were therefore converted to their cargo configuration and used in the airlift system from 8 February through 11 March 1968.[63/]

Personnel problems arising from the Tet Offensive were partly solved at the same time the shortage of airplanes was overcome, because units coming into the theatre from the United States brought with them their aircrews and nearly all of the required maintenance personnel. The situation was different for the 2d Aerial Port Group. Its workload had been increasing more rapidly than its manpower all through 1967, and when Tet came, additional personnel were urgently required. The crisis was met by the 60-day TDY assignment of 310 people to the Group from the 315th Air Division and the United States. Additional PCS personnel were programmed to replace them at the end of their TDY.[64/]

The problem of the degenerating priority system was less tractable. MACV tried to develop priorities within priorities but that proved unwieldy.[65/] An Ad Hoc Airlift Steering Committee was formed to consider the problem during mid-February. Officers from 7AF, USARV, 834th Air Division, Transportation Management Agency (TMA), and the J-45 section of MACV comprised the membership of the committee.[66/] It recommended that a contingency plan be developed to call in Military Airlift Command C-141s for work between the major ports, so as to help the tactical airlift forces overcome surge requirements. It also pointed at the sparsity of C-130 fields in the southern part of the Republic as a source of difficulty, and recommended that measures be taken to increase the use of truck and water transportation in that area to relieve some of the pressure on the airlift system. That, however, did not do much to solve the priority problem, and finally at the end of February, it was decided arbitrarily to return to preplanned and scheduled airlift missions.[67/]

Late in 1967, the number of C-130s in-country which would approach saturation of the facilities of the system was estimated to be about 54 airplanes.[68/] The graph in Figure 7 supports this statement, for the curve representing tons hauled per aircraft in-country reaches its nadir at about the time that the line representing the total number of aircraft reaches its zenith. From July 1967 to February 1968, the curve representing tons hauled per aircraft shows a steady decline, while that showing the numbers of aircraft in-country shows a steady rise. This may support the idea that the facilities tended to become saturated when more than 54 C-130s were in-country. The average number of C-130s in-country in August 1967 was 51.1, and in September the figure had risen to 56.1. The number then rose every month until May 1968, when it showed a very slight decline. The experience in March seems to contradict the generalization, because the amount of cargo carried rose despite the fact that the number of C-130s in-country was well above 54. A possible explanation for this might lie in the length of the crew duty day which was by regulation, 12 hours. In those days, the aircraft commander had the authority to extend the crew day as much as one hour, and the ALCC was permitted to extend it still further. It is possible that the facilities remained saturated in March, but the longer crew day caused the rise in tons hauled per airplane. Moreover, the TAC C-130s did not arrive until mid-February but they were available for the entire month of March. Since their Allowable Cabin Load (ACL) was greater than that of the C-7s, the C-123s, and many of the already-present C-130s, they were doubtless responsible for part of the March increase in tons hauled (Fig. 8) per airplane. From April through August 1968, the curves reversed themselves. The numbers of aircraft declined, the load on facilities moved away from saturation, and the amount of cargo carried by each aircraft increased. An examination of the curve for the rest of the year demonstrates that the generalization held true at least until December 1968.

The danger of saturation was recognized before the beginning of Tet, and steps were then underway to build a reserve capability. In a letter to General McLaughlin dated 23 January 1968, the Director of Operations of the 834th Air Division wrote that when construction of the west ramp at Cam Ranh Bay and "Charlie Row" at Tan Son Nhut were completed, the combined C-130 capacity of those two bases alone would be 111 airplanes.69/ He did caution, however, that this was a measure of parking space alone, and had nothing to do with the capacity of the Aerial Port Group or the maintenance organization needed to support that large a force.

The problem of the "domino effect" in the priority system has not yet been solved, and MACV is still using the priority system which was in effect on 31 January 1968. The level at which the domino effect occurs is, of course, related to the number of aircraft available, the facilities available for supporting these aircraft, and the magnitude of the emergency. In the time that has passed since Tet, a large number of new facilities have come into use, and TAC can bring a considerable number of C-130s into the theater on short order, though it is not a step to be taken lightly. Thus, the level at which emergency requests began their self-sustaining increase was higher by May 1969, than in February 1968, but still exists and the problem remains.

As was the case with the Khe Sanh campaign, responsiveness must be the ultimate criterion for the evaluation of the tactical airlift system's response to the Tet Offensive. In this regard, all of the Tactical Emergency requests and emergency resupply requests were filled; some combat essential and many lower priority requests were late. Since all emergency requests were fulfilled, it is probably fair to say the system was sufficiently responsive, but if it had possessed the resources to prevent saturation of facilities and to permit the on-time delivery of lower priority cargo, its responsiveness would have been greater.

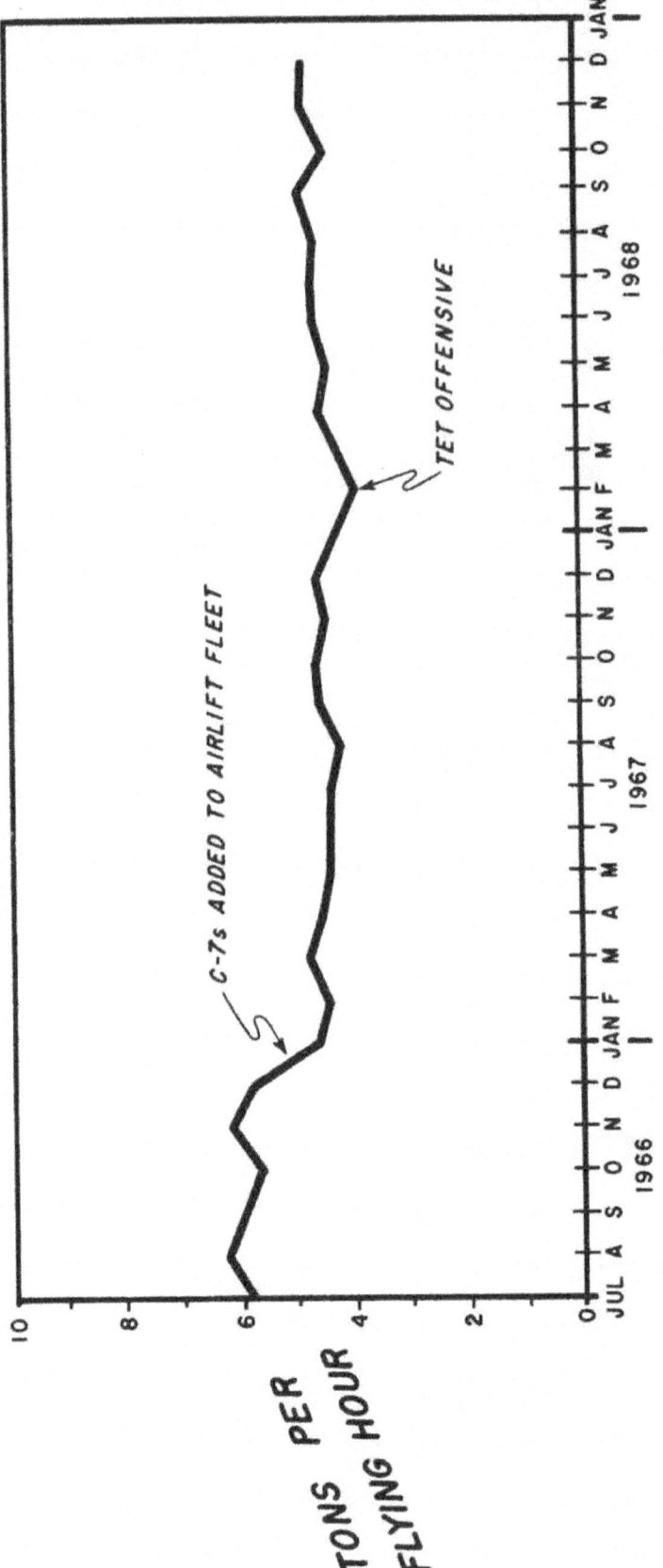

FIGURE 8

As for economy of force, Figure 8 illustrates that insofar as tons airlifted per flying hour are a measure, the effectiveness of the airlift organization reached its nadir during the Tet Offensive. In fairness, however, it should be noted, this drop in tons per flying hour was not indicative of a drop in tactical airlift efficiency, but rather a decrease of the airlift fleet's productiveness due to overriding factors. The expanding tactical situation in I Corps, including Khe Sanh, increased the number of fighters, recon, and airlift aircraft responding to requirements in that area. This heavy influx of air traffic into northern RVN, in addition to adverse weather conditions during this period, saturated the controlled airspace, and overtaxed the traffic control agencies. Priority for through or terminating traffic was naturally given to jet aircraft which resulted in increased hours per sortie for airlift aircraft. The expanded airlift requirements into the I Corps Tactical Zone also increased sortie lengths throughout the airlift fleet. Ground attacks against onload airfields frequently disrupted airlift operations, imposing delays in loading, refueling, etc. It was also not uncommon during this period, to have a launched aircraft fail to complete a given sortie, due to the intended offload base being under ground attack upon its arrival. Increased sortie length, delays attributed to airspace saturation, the tactical situation, and adverse weather conditions were factors which reduced tonnage productiveness per hour.

Operation DELAWARE, which started on 19 April and continued until 17 May, was another battle in which the airlift forces played a significant role. The purpose of the operation was to disrupt a major enemy supply route and to destroy as much of his materiel as possible.

Operation DELAWARE took place in the remote A Shau Valley near the Laotian border. The valley is located about 25 miles southwest of Hue, and it runs from northwest to southeast. It is about 15 miles long, and its floor is about 2,000 feet above sea level. The ridges on both sides of the valley rise some 4,000 feet about sea level, and there is a peak about five miles beyond the northern end of the valley which reaches nearly 6,000 feet. The floor of the valley has considerable open space, but the ridges are heavily wooded. There is a small airstrip at the northern end of the A Shau called A Luoi, and the DZ was located immediately to the south of the field. The airfield is on the eastern side of the valley, and the crest of the ridge to the west is about four miles away from it.

The original Army plan was to capture the A Luoi airfield on the second day of the operation and clear it rapidly enough to permit C-7 landings on the fifth day and C-123 operations on the sixth. Meanwhile, the force was to have been supplied by means of helicopters and airdrops. The C-130s were to have maintained a three-day level of supplies by dropping 225 tons a day from the third day to the sixth. 70/

The operation ran behind schedule and the airport was not captured until the day the C-123s were to have begun their landings. The restoration of the field could not even begin until the tenth day, and thus the drops on the part of the C-130s became much more important and far more extensive than had been required in the original plan. To further complicate the

the situation, the plan had called for importation of a portable GCA unit by helicopter. The equipment was not brought in until after a period of bad weather conditions had passed; thus, the C-130s had to rely upon their own means of navigation.[71/] The GCA requirement would not have been of crucial significance had the weather been as good as was expected at that time of year. That was not to be, however, and helicopter operations were severely curtailed, thus placing a heavier load on the C-130s at the very time they were called upon to make airborne radar approaches to a DZ hidden in a valley surrounded by some very rugged terrain. The bad weather condition also made it impossible to give proper fighter cover to the drop missions.[72/]

It was known that the enemy had large anti-aircraft weapons on hand, and it was suspected some of these might even be radar controlled. Both 23-mm and 37-mm guns were definitely identified, and it was thought some 57-mm weapons were in place along the Laotian border.

Confirming the enemy had many anti-aircraft emplacements in the southern end of the valley, a C-130B of the 315th Air Division, commanded by Maj. Liliburn Stow, was hit by fire on its final run into the DZ. The aircraft was carrying a load of ammunition which was set afire; the cargo exploded immediately after the airplane hit the ground. All crewmembers were killed, along with two combat photographers of the 600th Photo Squadron, who were on board.[73/]

Subsequent aircraft were further warned about the heavy weapons and attempts were made to bring arriving aircraft into the valley north of the gun emplacements. Nevertheless, several of the aircraft were severely damaged. One C-130E had the outboard half of its horizontal stabilizer shot away, and a "B Model" suffered a hole in its wing that was big enough for man to jump through.

Results of the A Shau Valley attack indicated that by April the airlift system had more than recovered from the Tet Offensive. Maj. Gen. John J. Tolson, Commanding General of the U.S. Army's 1st Cavalry Division, said in a letter:[74/]

> "On 26 and 27 April in the A Shau Valley, I witnessed your C-130 crews in one of the most magnificent displays of courage and airmanship I have ever seen. The low ceilings, mountainous terrain, lack of terminal navigation facilities and enemy anti-aircraft fire all combined to create an exceedingly hazardous environment for the planned resupply drops.... I strongly recommend that suitable awards for valor be presented to each member of the crews involved...."

Though the original plan had called for only six days of drops at a rate of 225 tons per day, it was necessary to continue the C-130 operations for nine days, and the average amount of cargo delivered was 238 tons per day. Partly because of the effectiveness of airlift support, DELAWARE was a success. The enemy lost almost a thousand men and a large amount of materiel, including 12 37-mm anti-aircraft guns.[75/]

Before the termination of Operation DELAWARE, another crisis arose to test the responsiveness of the tactical airlift forces in Southeast Asia: the evacuation of Kham Duc, a Special Forces Camp which was located about 60 miles to the southeast of the A Shau Valley, due west of Chu Lai, and just ten miles from the Laotian border. The site was in a valley surrounded by rough terrain and, fortunately, included a runway capable of handling the C-130.

The camp had been under increasing pressure from the enemy since the early hours of 10 May 1968 and Gen. William C. Westmoreland, the MACV Commander, made the decision to evacuate it early on the morning of the 12th. Headquarters, Seventh Air Force, was notified at 0605 hours and by 1000 hours the first aircraft, a C-130, landed at Kham Duc. Thirty-seven minutes later, there were three C-130s and one C-123 orbiting overhead awaiting their turns to go in between friendly airstrikes and enemy mortar attacks.[76/] Unfortunately, the first C-130 suffered a flat tire and could take no passengers out of Kham Duc. The second aircraft, a C-123, landed at 1105 hours and took off just three minutes later with the first load of 66 evacuees.[77/] It was decided that the C-130 with the blown tire could not be repaired on the spot because of the continuing enemy attack, and that it would have to be flown out without repairs. The mission commander, who later stated that he understood there would be no more fixed-wing landings at Kham Duc, decided to extract the combat control team on that aircraft which departed at about 1300.[78/]

A total of eight C-130s and three C-123s landed at Kham Duc that day, all of them under intense ground fire and with the help of maximum-effort close air support. About 529 American and Vietnamese troops were evacuated on five C-130 sorties and one C-123 sortie.[79/] Another 150 persons were lost with the crew of a C-130 commanded by Maj. Bernard Bucher when it was shot down on takeoff at about 1530 hours.[80/] About an hour later, the combat control team and mission commander, having been ordered to return to Kham Duc, arrived on board a C-130. They investigated the camp and found the evacuation was complete.

The Forward Air Controller (FAC) nearly delivered a strike to destroy a C-130 which had earlier left the runway and been so damaged that it could not be brought out. A C-130 pilot warned him that the combat control team was still on the ground, so the FAC held up the strikes and made arrangements for the rescue. [81/]

A C-123 landed in the midst of heavy ground fire and the crew did not see anyone, so began their takeoff roll, whereupon the combat control team jumped up from their hiding place to signal the aircraft. It was too late to stop, so the crew continued their takeoff and advised the FAC that there were indeed some Americans on the ground. Since the airplane was running low on fuel, a second C-123, under the Command of Lt. Col. Joe M. Jackson, was sent in. [82/] The landing was made under a hail of fire; the leader of the combat control team said by that time there were 50 caliber guns in place at each end of the runway. The team leaped out of their hiding place in a culvert and, firing their M-16s at the 50 caliber guns as they ran, boarded the C-123; the pilot immediately took off through heavy small arms, rocket, and mortar fire. [83/] Colonel Jackson was later awarded the Congressional Medal of Honor for his part in the action. [84/]

The work of the airlift crews at Kham Duc was outstanding. The 529 lives were saved at the price of two C-130s, the lives of one aircrew, and those of 150 passengers. [85/] The price was costly enough but it might easily have been higher. In the words of Lt. Col. Robert B. Nelson, Commander of the Army troops involved: [86/]

> "On behalf of the officers and men of the 2d Battalion, 1st Infantry, I would like to extend our deepest appreciation for the heroic actions of the men of your command (834th Air Division) who participated in the extraction of the Kham Duc Special Forces Camp on 12 May 1968. Their absolute disregard of the imminent danger and their dedication to their mission is a tribute to their professional competence and individual courage. Were it not for the C-130 pilots of the 834th Air Division, the ground elements would never have completed the extraction and many more American lives would have been lost."

The partial bombing halt in the spring of 1968 and the opening of the Paris peace talks were reflected in the activities of the airlift system. The workload leveled off at about 130,000 tons a month and it was possible to reduce the number of aircraft in-country. By December there were hardly more than 200 of them under operational control of the 834th.[87/] Though the level of operations did not decline appreciably, the level of violence did for there were no more Kham Ducs in 1968. Worthy of mention is Operation GOLDEN SWORD--it involved more than 500 sorties. More than 5,200 passengers and 1,740 tons of cargo were hauled from Hue to Bien Hoa during September. LIBERTY CANYON was the name of the operation which moved the entire 1st Air Cavalry Division from Quang Tri and Camp Evans south to Quan Loi, Song Be, and Tay Ninh. This movement involved 11,500 troops and 3,600 tons of cargo, which were moved during October and November 1968, by 473 sorties.[88/]

Throughout this reporting period, the Special Forces system was heavily dependent, not only on tactical air support in times of crises, but also upon the tactical airlift system for its daily bread and butter. During the last half of 1968, the Special Forces camps received more than

80 percent of their supplies from the air lines of communication and the balance from waterborne transportation. Without the airlines of communication, the entire Special Forces organization could not have existed. The greater part of the work was done by C-7s because runways at the majority of the camps were too small to accommodate the C-130 or even the C-123. 89/ As in the case with most forward bases, there has been little back-haul cargo generated by the Special Forces camps. The idle airlift capability has often been used to good effect in terms of Civic Action.

Many Vietnamese rural residents have been carried, after they have been cleared by the province chief, to the cities, so they might visit relatives or buy provisions. This seems to have done some good by winning favorable publicity for the Government of Vietnam. A suggestion has been projected that after the termination of hostilities, it might be wise for the United States to provide, in a controlled way, some airlift capability to the Government of Vietnam. This might help to strengthen the ties between the rural areas and Saigon. 90/

Figure 6 shows the number of TE, ER, and CE requests fulfilled by the airlift system during the period of the report; however, such data were really no measure of the responsiveness of the organization. Responsiveness was necessarily difficult to quantify, because it was so strongly influenced by a "feeling" on the part of the user. This feeling was probably at a low ebb at the very time when the airlift system was servicing approximately six times the number of requests as had been usual in the months preceding Tet.

Lt.Col. Lawrence W. Whitney, USA, Chief, J-4 Branch, MACV, who might be considered a representative of all the users, believed the airlift organization was extremely responsive. He said it fulfilled all Tactical Emergency and Emergency Resupply Requests levied upon it. The Combat Essential Requests were on time in the very great majority of cases, and where the Required Delivery Date had been missed, it had been due to foul weather, maintenance breakdown, or saturation of the forward air fields. He also said that the great increase in the number of emergency requests at the time of Tet certainly did cause a considerable increase in the levels of normal cargo backlogged in the aerial ports and this added to the number of emergency requests. Colonel Whitney added that the priority system in mid-1969 was essentially the same as it was at the time of Tet, except for a procedure which was implemented at MACV in May of 1968 to combat the tendency of the system to fall into a situation wherein the emergency requests would be generated at a runaway rate. A certain arbitrary level was selected and when the requests reached that point, MACV J-4 began to take an especially hard look at the "essentiality" of the requests and was even more reluctant than usual to accept the validity of the requests. Even where the "essentiality" of the goods in question was granted, J-4 sometimes scaled down the size of the request with the assurance to the user that if the normal priority system did not produce the materiel in question before the emergency supplies were again running low, then another emergency shipment would be made.[91/]

The citations of a very great number of users could be added: then Secretary of the Air Force Hon. Harold Brown, Generals William C. Westmoreland, USAF, Robert S. Cushman, USMC, and William W. Momyer, USAF, and many other distinguished officials have commented on the responsiveness of the airlift system.[92/]

CHAPTER II

COMMAND AND CONTROL PROBLEMS

To control airlift forces, adherence to organizational procedures is essential (Fig. 9). In the initial action, the user in the field issues a request for delivery of supplies, including a Required Date of Delivery (DOD). This request is sent through Division and Field Force headquarters, until it reaches the MACV Command Center. The J-4 (Logistics) section of this center passes on its validity; if it is approved, the Airlift Control Center (ALCC) receives it. If disapproved, the request is returned down the chain of command to the user; the originator has an opportunity to formulate a request for transportation by some other means.

Once the J-4 section has approved a request, it becomes mandatory for the airlift system to fulfill it. The scheduling section of the Airlift Control Center, with the advice of the Director of Traffic Operations (an Aerial Port Group representative stationed in the ALCC), develops the daily orders designed to fulfill all approved requests on or before their Required Delivery Dates. Once the daily order is written, it is sent to the various ALCEs and Aerial Ports for their comments before it is put into final form. Modifications to the order are made if the subordinate units make valid suggestions or objections, and it is sent out as a "frag" (daily operations or "fragmentary" order) to the various Tactical Unit Operations Centers (TUOCs) or their equivalents on the evening before it is to be executed.

The TUOCs then schedule aircraft and crews against the "frag" and carry out whatever other operations and maintenance functions are required to meet the schedule. Once the aircraft depart the station on their first sortie, they are under operational control of the ALCC, until they return at the end of the "frag" or the end of the crew day, whichever comes first. At the time of the initial takeoff, the ALCC begins to flight-follow every aircraft, using information given it by the aircrew, either directly on the HF radio or through the Airlift Control Elements (ALCEs), transportable ALCEs, or the Combat Control Teams (CCTs) using VHF or UHF. Besides acting as communications links, the last three named units must coordinate matters at their stations, and act as the controlling agency of all 834th Air Division airplanes while they are on the ground.[1/]

This system operates satisfactorily, although it is easy to find individual citations that would indicate the contrary. There are frequent legs flown with empty or partly filled aircraft but that is, as was pointed out in Chapter I, inherent in any tactical airlift system. At the end of 1968, the scheduling of missions was still being done manually, though plans were being implemented to automate the process. Some interim efforts had been made to improve the efficiency of the manual process; for example, after the fragmentary orders were completed in the afternoon of the day preceding the operations in question, they were sent to the various ALCEs and aerial port units. This enabled them to make comments or offer suggestions for improvements in the next

# COMMAND & CONTROL ORGANIZATION

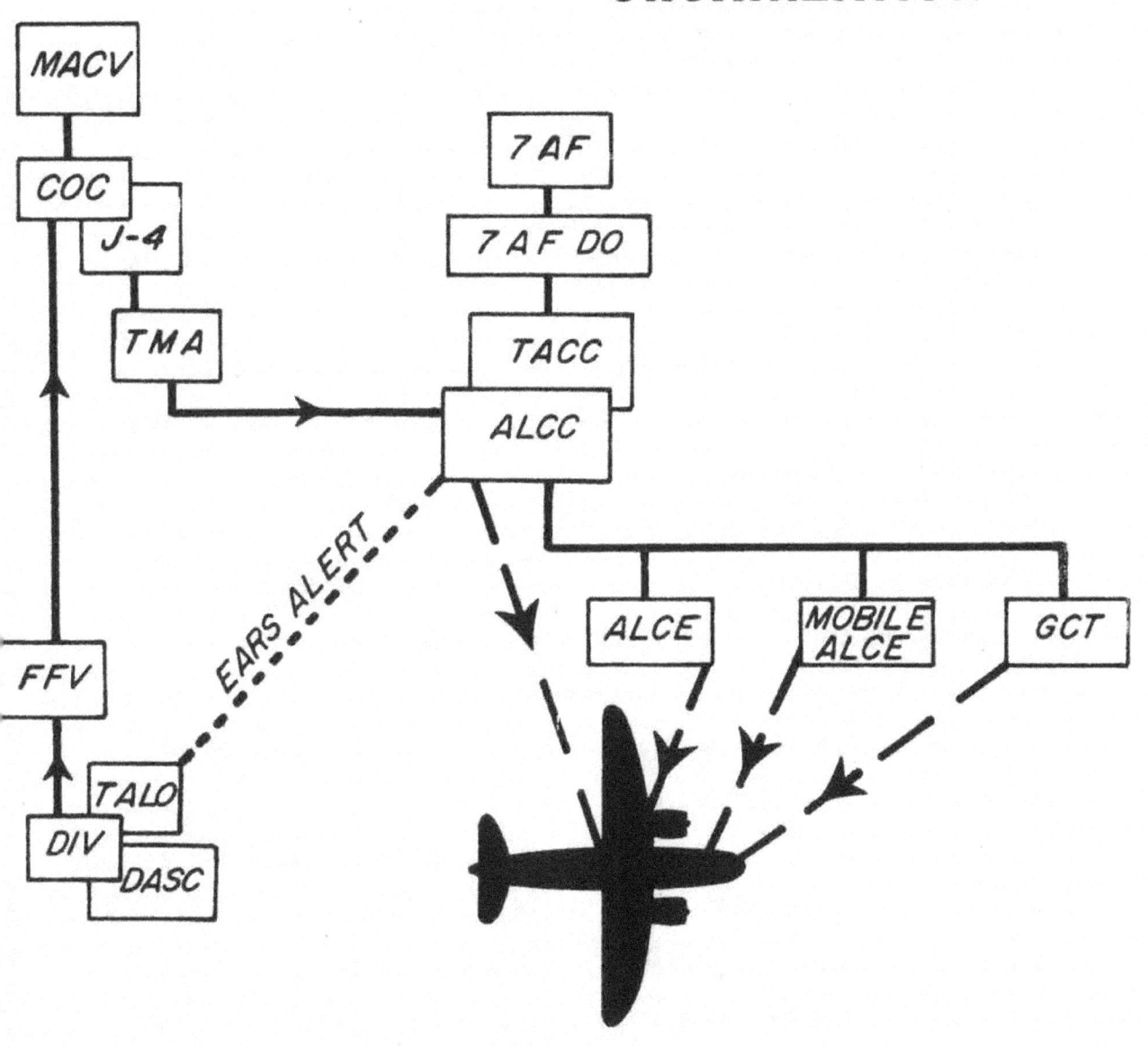

FIGURE 9

day's orders. During the Tet Offensive, attempts were made through scheduling arising out of saturation of facilities. The number of night missions were increased for the C-130s allowing the load on aerial ports to be more evenly distributed, since the C-123s and C-7s could be used only during the daylight hours.[2/] Of some help, a 7AF computer study suggested the optimum mix of C-123s and C-130s in carrying out the scheduled passenger missions should be five C-130s and eight C-123s scheduled daily. This was advisable because the C-123 reaches its maximum passenger and weight capacity simultaneously, while the C-130 is using only about half of its weight-carrying ability when it has a full load of passengers.[3/]

Establishing this command and control system was not a painless process. In unifying the system, the uncertain political climate, insecure environment in which communications facilities operated, manpower ceilings, shortage of equipment, inexperienced ground and aircrew personnel, and the need to reconcile the control structure with Air Force doctrine, had to be considered.

The command and control system described here is not consistent with that prescribed in AFM 2-7, Tactical Air Control System. It states the ALCC is subordinate to TACC, and TACC will control all aircraft.[4/] In SEA, however, circumstances dictated a diversion from the doctrine appearing in AFM 2-7. As General McLaughlin stated in his End of Tour Report, TACC simply did not possess the manpower, skills, and facilities to absorb an airlift mission workload which was larger than the fighter/

recon workload. As a result, the ALCC assumed complete control function over all tactical airlift, placing it lateral (except in overall airspace control and high threat determination), rather than subordinate to TACC. General McLaughlin believed that, since the present structure in SEA has been fully justified, the basic doctrine should be modified to permit the Air Force component commander the flexibility to either combine or separate functions of the TACC and the ALCC.[5/] Combining the TACC/ALCC functions is still a valid concept in operations of smaller scope or shorter duration, and provides an initial departure point for large scale, long duration operations such as those in Vietnam.

A C-7 liaison office was established at Tan Son Nhut during the summer of 1967 to perform the functions which AFM 2-7 assigns to ALCEs. This inconsistency was appreciated at the time but the office was needed because of the geographical separation of the ALCE and the C-7 ramp, the shortage of ALCE personnel (the unit was manned out of 483d TAW resources), and because of the difficulty of finding sufficient opportune cargo to fully utilize the C-7 airlift capacity.[6/] In April 1969, the functions of that liaison office were being absorbed by the Tan Son Nhut ALCE.

Perhaps the most serious obstacle to be overcome was the lack of communications facilities suitable for following and coordinating more than a thousand flights every day.[7/] At first, the airlift system did not possess its own net, the insecure land lines were unreliable, communications discipline was difficult to instill in the crews, and the airlift forces had to compete with many other units for the needed facilities and equipment.[8/] During February 1967, the Chief of Staff, USAF approved three nets for the 834th Air Division: UHF air-to-ground, Single Side Band HF, and secure teletype.[9/] The equipment was acquired and the system was gradually built up, until the ALCEs had most of the equipment programmed by the end of 1968. The system was working quite well, though it was occasionally necessary to remind the aircrews of their responsibilities for transmitting data back to the ALCC to enable that unit to fulfill its duties of flight following, coordination, and control.[10/] During a crisis, as at Khe Sanh, insecure communications could be very damaging.[11/] This particular problem had been recognized very early and Project SEEK SILENCE was implemented to overcome it. It called for installation of a secure voice capability in all airlift aircraft and associated controlling agencies on the ground. Progress in acquiring the necessary modifications/equipment, however, has been slow, as many people believe the airlift mission does not warrant this expensive equipment. Additional pressure has been exerted by MACV, however, for the release of funds to make this modification readily available. Presently, a small percentage of the airlift fleet has been modified to accept the new equipment, but until ground agencies have also been modified, no "black boxes" will be released, nor can an estimated completion date be established.[12/]

Tactical Airlift Liaison Officers (TALOs) were attached to the Tactical Air Control Parties deployed with the field forces during late

47

1966. This turned out very well for it was possible for the TALOs to brief the ground commander on better utilization of the airlift resources, and to coordinate airlift movements to save much wasted time and motion.[13/] The addition of a Traffic Management Officer, later to be called the Director of Traffic Operations, did much to improve the coordination of Aerial Port affairs within the Airlift Control Center.[14/]

An air transportable ALCE was satisfactorily tested at Quang Tri and Ban Me Thout during the summer of 1968. All necessary facilities for a complete ALCE can be airlifted by two C-130s.[15/] It consists of three air-conditioned modules: (1) Command Shelter--radio communication equipment and status boards necessary to control an airlift operation; (2) Sleeping Shelter--provides bunks for 42 people; and (3) Sanitary Shelter--has 12 facilities, including washers and driers, and showers for the convenience of personnel. Two additional units are being procured and scheduled for delivery during the latter part of FY70.[16/]

Even though the communications nets were fairly complete by the end of 1968, they were not wholly satisfactory not only for the reasons listed, but also because they were not fast enough. The leaders of the airlift system have long desired automated communications so as to make possible more timely transmission of data, decision-making, and delivery of orders.[17/] Proposals for a system which would provide for the instantaneous, secure transmission and processing of data were made during the spring of 1967; the idea was approved that summer, and a development program was started soon after.[18/]

The result has been the SEEK DATA II Program, which provides a central computer to manage the airlift operation. This system will receive data from TMA and the aerial ports on each airlift request. It will match these requirements with available airlift resources, considering the priority, RDD, dimensions, and destination of each request. From these data and up-to-the-minute information received on each take-off and landing, the computer will be able to automatically frag, schedule, and flight-follow the entire airlift operation in Vietnam. The Control Data Corporation is presently working on the computer programs required to support SEEK DATA II; however, the IBM 360/50 computer needed to handle the airlift portion of this program is not yet available (awaiting approval from OSD).[19]

Two improved communications systems utilizing AUTODIN and UYA-7s are planned. These systems will support the SEEK DATA II Automated Management System by providing real time, secure digital communications between the ALCEs, Aerial Port Squadrons, forward operating locations, and the ALCC.[20] Sixteen dedicated AUTODIN terminals--located at the ALCC, at each of the established ALCEs, and the three major aerial port squadrons--are programmed. Twenty-three UYA-7 terminals are being procured for use with HF/SSB radios. These units will provide communications between forward operating locations and the ALCEs at Da Nang, Cam Ranh Bay, and Tan Son Nhut. The UYA-7s will form three separate HF radio networks and interface with the AUTODIN system.[21]

The Emergency Air Request System had its origin in the fall of 1966 when the first tests were conducted.[22] They were successful and, though the system had been refined slightly, it was essentially the same at the end of 1968. In 1966, the 834th Air Division and 7AF believed the system required a dedicated communications net, but MACV did not agree and the organic communications of the requestor's chain of command are still in use.[23]

The commander requiring emergency airlift service initiates a request, which includes a Required Delivery Date, and it is passed up through his chain of command to the division level. Tactical Airlift Liaison Officers (TALOs) are assigned at that level, and they immediately use their own communications net to alert the ALCC of the impending request, so that the latter can begin planning for the move should it be approved. Meanwhile, the request continues up through the chain of command, until it arrives at the J-4 section of MACV. As it continues to be processed, silence at lower command levels implies their consent. From the time a Tactical Emergency or Emergency Resupply request arrives at ALCC, the command has two hours to allow an airplane to arrive at the onload station ready for the mission. A Combat Essential request allows eight hours.[24]

The Emergency Airlift Request System has, according to Lt. Col. L. W. Whitney, USA, Chief, J-4 Branch, MACV, worked very well under most conditions. He said that during Tet, it bore up under the strain, as the normal priority system was modified a little to insure the vast number of vital emergency moves were being carried out first.[25/]

Contributing to the success of the Emergency Airlift Request System was the C-7A, a light, airlift aircraft which had the capability of operating from fields which could not accommodate larger airlift aircraft. The C-7A was originally acquired for the U.S. Army and was designed to land and take off on strips less than a thousand feet long; however, Air Force regulations restricted its use to those fields having at least a thousand feet or more of runway. As of 31 January 1969, there were 40 strips in SVN where the C-7A could be used, but which were inadequate for the larger C-123 and C-130 aircraft.[26/] During 1967 and 1968, this aircraft carried an average payload of about 1.4 tons per sortie.

The agreement which governed the transfer of the C-7 fleet from the Army to the Air Force states:[27/]

> "A. The Chief of Staff U.S. Army (CSA) agrees to relinquish all claims for CV-2 and CV-7 aircraft and for future fixed-wing aircraft designed for tactical airlift. Those assets now in the Army inventory will be transferred to the Air Force. (CSA and CSAF agree that this does not apply to administrative mission support fixed-wing aircraft.)
>
> "B. The Chief of Staff U.S. Air Force (CSAF) agrees:
> (1) To relinquish all claims for helicopters and follow-on rotary-wing aircraft which are designed and operated for intratheater movement, fire support, supply and resupply of Army Forces and those Air Force control elements assigned to DASC and subordinate thereto. (CSA and CSAF agree that this does not include rotary-wing aircraft employed by Air Force SAW and SAR forces and rotary-wing administrative mission support aircraft.) CSA and CSAF agree that the Army and Air Force jointly will continue to develop

VTOL aircraft. Dependent upon the evolution of this type aircraft, methods of employment and control will be matters for continuing joint consideration by the Army and Air Force.

(2) That in cases of operational need the CV-2, CV-7 and C-123 type aircraft performing supply/resupply or troop-lift functions in the field army area may be attached to the subordinate tactical echelons of the field army (Corps, Division, or subordinate commander as determined by the appropriate joint/unified commander). Note: Authority for attachment is established by Subsection 6, Section 2 of JCS Pub 2, Unified Action Armed Forces (UNAAF).

(3) To retain the CV-2 and CV-7 aircraft in the Air Force Structure and to consult with the Chief of Staff U.S. Army prior to changing the force levels of replacing these aircraft.

(4) To consult with the Chief of Staff U.S. Army in order to arrive at take off, landing and load carrying characteristics of follow-on fixed wing aircraft to meet the needs of the Army for supply, resupply and troop movement functions.

"C. The Chief of Staff, U.S. Army, and the Chief of Staff, U.S. Air Force, jointly agree:

(1) To revise all service doctrinal statements, manuals and other material in variance with the substance and spirit of this agreement.

(2) That the necessary actions resulting from this agreement will be completed by 1 January 1967."

The agreement permitted the airlift resources to be used in a dedicated (as opposed to a common service) fashion, and that is the way in which the Army had been using the C-7s. They had been deployed in six aviation companies at different locations in South Vietnam, and were under the operational control of various ground force commanders. In the opinion of Col. Paul J. Mascot, USAF, the first Commander of the 483d Tactical Airlift Wing, the Army's philosophy of operations is different from that of the Air Force. He said, "I had (by January

UNCLASSIFIED
C-7A CARIBOU

FIGURE 10

1967) already become aware that under Army control our Air Force pilots' training and procedures for in-country check outs were inadequate.... Crews, falling into the Army attitude regarding mission priority, had accepted the many hazards to safe aircraft operations as necessary to get the job done."[28/] The transition, then, was not a sudden one, but rather Air Force crew members and ground personnel were on hand in-country learning the operation from the Army for some months before the transfer became effective. In fact, the 483d Tactical Airlift Wing (TAW) was officially activated at Cam Ranh Bay by 15 October 1966, though it did not assume control of the aircraft until the beginning of the next year.

The Wing Headquarters, along with two of the flying squadrons and a consolidated maintenance squadron, was located at Cam Ranh Bay, while two of the other squadrons were at Vung Tau. The last two were assigned to the Phu Cat Air Base then under construction a few miles to the northwest of Qui Nhon.[29/]

It was decided that at first, at least, no changes would be made in the Army's mode of operation. The dedicated service would be continued until the need for change became apparent.[30/]

Insofar as command and control are concerned, the principal problems were a perennial personnel crisis, the difficulty of maintaining an adequate flying safety program in an area of high accident potential, and the need to make the operation as efficient as possible by using as much of the Allowable Cabin Load (ACL) as could be arranged on all sorties. Traffic control at forward fields and the poor artillery warning system constituted problems which were equally grave.

The personnel problems of the C-7 organization have been very critical for several reasons. First, nearly all personnel in the Wing (having been organized in-country) were scheduled to rotate at nearly the same time; this came to be a cyclic problem every year, with the experience level of the crew members reaching a peak in September or October, and then declining very rapidly until it reached its low point during the early part of the winter.[31/] Secondly, the one year tour length was detrimental to the continuity of the training and flying safety programs. This unstable personnel situation was further aggravated by the fact that the outbound person's date of departure was relatively fixed, while the inbound man might appear at any time within the programmed month or, quite often, in the succeeding month. This was often caused by backlogs of personnel awaiting entry to the Jungle Survival School at Clark Air Base, Philippines, or the difficulty in obtaining transportation to Vietnam after the completion of the School.[32/]

At various times during the two years considered, the output in flight engineers of the Combat Crew Training School at Sewart AFB, Tenn., declined due to unprogrammed attrition and this also compounded the personnel problem. Moreover, the engineers were playing a dual role, since they also served as loadmasters. This was particularly fatiguing in the C-7, which required much more unloading and loading than in the C-123s and C-130s, because of the shorter sortie length. Cargo handling equipment for C-123s and C-130s was also more efficient and thus required less muscle power. 33/

To overcome these difficulties, a request was made to have loadmasters assigned to the C-7s. 34/ It was believed this would add to the efficiency of the operation, despite the fact that the weight of the loadmaster would subtract from the ACL. 35/ Although this request was not approved, other measures were taken to relieve the chronic engineer shortage. By the fall of 1968, the flight surgeon had stated it was detrimental to flying safety. 36/

Measures taken were to order TDY personnel to the Wing and use crew chiefs as engineers. This latter step was not altogether satisfactory, since it was detrimental to the maintenance program. Some relief was also achieved by increasing the input to the school at Sewart, and ordering some panel engineers to proceed direct to Vietnam without attending the Combat Crew Training School. 37/

The number of pilots assigned to the C-7 Wing was never as great a problem as in the case of the engineers. During mid-1968, however, a crisis was created when PACAF decided the 483d had an excess of pilots and that 31 of them would have to be used in other jobs. This, along with the Air Force requirement that a pilot remain in the cockpit for the first five years out of flying school, might have decimated the ranks of the unit's aircraft commanders and have lowered the experience level to an unacceptable level. Headquarters Air Force lessened the impact of the move, however, by allowing some of the junior men to be transferred. 38/

The acquisition of the C-7A aircraft designed with a supershort field capability (compared to other Air Force inventory fixed-wing aircraft), placed Air Force pilots in an environment demanding the utmost in skill and judgment. Immediately after activation, the 483d Tactical Airlift Wing initiated aircrew procedures to establish and maintain a high standard of effectiveness and safety.[39/] All newly assigned pilots were required to fly as copilots on several missions prior to receiving an Aircraft Commander's checkout. All aircraft commanders received periodic flight checks to insure continuing high standards. The short field takeoff and landing procedures were reserved for those fields actually requiring their use. The quality of the aircrew pre-mission briefing was improved, and the pilots were able to evaluate the relative priority of their mission, and the urgency of the delivery while weighing the environmental risk. A standard Air Force type aircraft check list was developed to replace those utilized by the U.S. Army personnel.[40/]

Another vexing problem faced by the 483d was the difficulty in utilizing all of the ACL on each sortie.[41/] As was pointed out, the average payload was approximately 1.4 tons per sortie, while the capability of the airplane was such that it could have hauled as much as 2.5 tons on each flight. In a tactical situation, some wasted motion is inevitable when so much of the cargo going out to the forward fields is in the form of expendables such as ammunition or food. Yet, because it was not a part of the common service user system, there had been a tendency to neglect use of the C-7 at the larger terminals. Accordingly, special efforts were begun to generate opportune cargo and expedite turnarounds. As was mentioned in Chapter I, a liaison office was installed at Tan Son Nhut and officers were sometimes sent to other terminals to improve C-7 utilization.[42/] The aircraft commanders were also indoctrinated to seek out opportune cargo wherever possible.[43/]

This was a difficult problem, because the Caribou could not hope to compete with the C-130s and C-123s for opportune cargo. One obvious reason for this was because aerial ports could not plan their palletization activities on an opportune basis. This work had to be done in advance, and since the greater part of the cargo was moved by aircraft using the 463L Material Handling Equipment, and since the C-7 was not compatible with that system, large amounts of cargo available for opportune movement with the C-7 could never be anticipated.

The aerial ports, as shorthanded as they are, will probably continue to find it easier to ship goods on the larger aircraft whenever there is a choice. MACV, in fact, took action to insure that C-7As would not be used in such a way as to compete with the other aircraft for the available cargo, when it instructed the appropriate commanders to send the C-7s only to those fields which were beyond the capabilities of the C-123 and C-130.[44/] Ultimately, the C-7's primary reason for being is responsiveness--to service those 40 fields in South Vietnam which cannot be reached by C-123s or C-130s.[45/]

As Figure 11 depicts, the Wing required a brief adjustment period. Statistics for Flying Hours and Tonnage Moved dropped below the previous average. However, after this short adjustment period, the beefed-up maintenance organizations and zealous endeavors of all Wing personnel turned the curve upward. The Wing's continuing high standard of performance is a testimonial to their determination and effectiveness of Air Force operational and management principles.

The Army-Air Force agreement cited here permitted the C-7s and even the C-123s to be used in a dedicated way as an alternate to the common service system.[46/] The initial Air Force philosophy of operation was to continue with the dedicated service. There has been a gradual increase in the number of C-7s changed over to the common service system, but the total number used that way is still very small.[47/] General Moore, in his End-of-Tour Report, recommended that though the Air Force has generally preferred a common service system, there does seem to be a need for dedicated service in Vietnam and that the C-7s should be continued to be used in that manner.[48/] General McLaughlin, General Moore's successor as Commander of the 834th Air Division, believed the commitment to the dedicated service system ought to be continued, and that the using commanders whould be made more responsible for the efficient use of the aircraft.[49/]

Many of the problems experienced in the operation of the C-7s were similar to those which arose in the use of the larger C-123. The C-123 is also a reciprocating two-engine, high wing, transport aircraft.

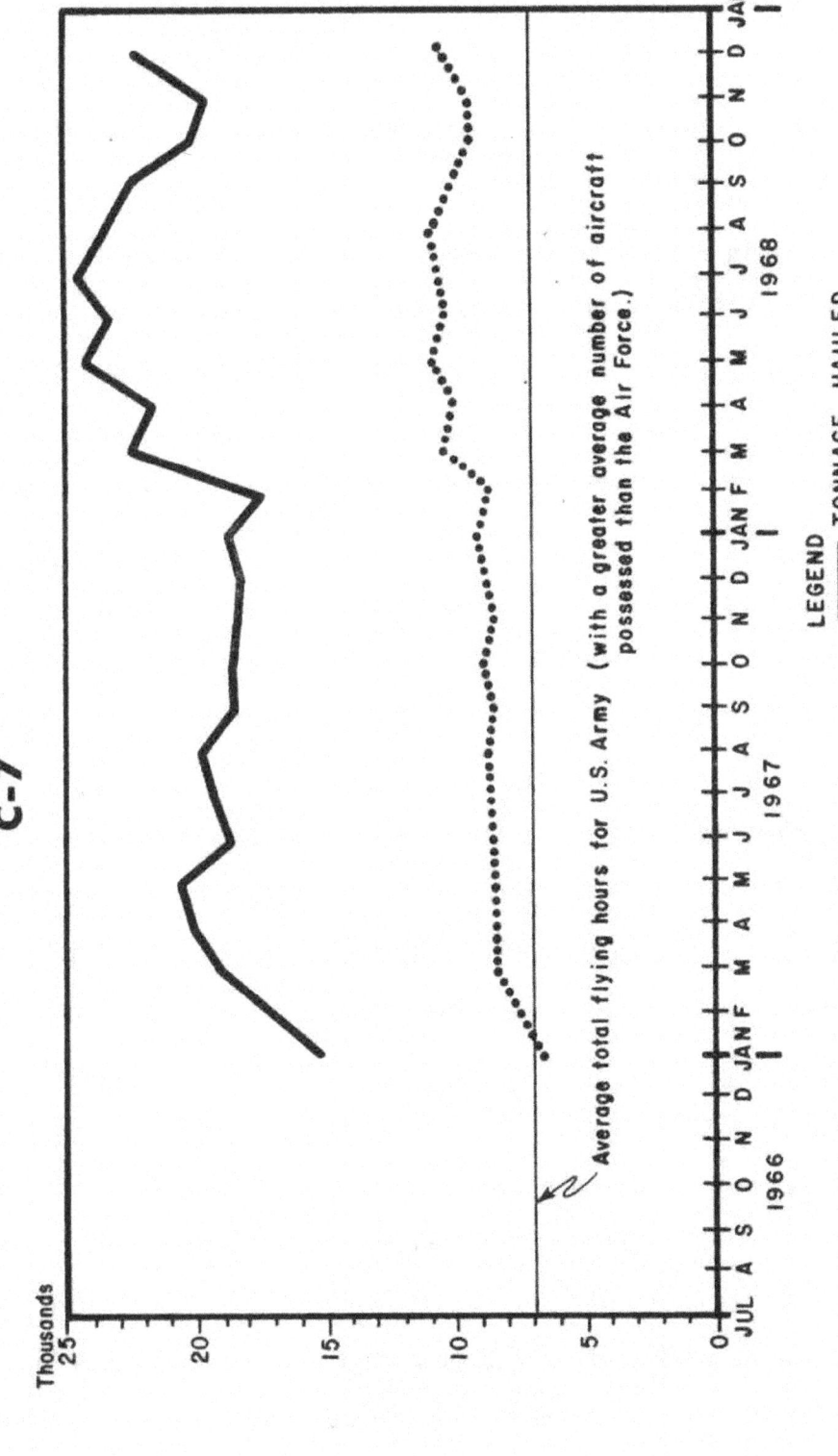

FIGURE 11

All of those currently in use in Vietnam have recently had two jet engines installed to improve their takeoff performance and their survivability in a hostile environment. The average tonnage of C-123s carried per flying hour (considering the 30-month period) has been 3.9 tons as compared with 2.2 for the C-7 and 7.5 for the C-130s. 50/

The 315th Special Operations Wing (SOW) experienced problems similar to those of the 483d TAW. There was a chronic shortage in the number of engineers and pilots assigned. 51/ Although the pilot shortage had eased somewhat by the summer of 1968, the shortage of engineers continued to exist. Many of the reasons for this shortage in the 315th SOW at Phan Rang, were much the same as those experienced by the 483d TAW at Cam Ranh Bay.

During mid-1967, the pilot shortage was eased when the Victory Squadron of the Royal Thailand Air Force (RTAF) began flying with the 19th Air Commando Squadron (later known as the 19th Special Operations Squadron). Such things as the diversion of inbound pilots to other jobs within SVN and late arrivals, continued to cause trouble until the beginning of FY 1969. 52/ There were also some problems in terms of experience. By 1968, many of the Air Force's older captains and younger majors, who were at the very peak of their flying proficiency, had already finished their tours and gone back to the United States. Lieutenant Colonels, who had just come from extended tours in jobs unrelated to flying, and young lieutenants who had just come from the pilot training schools, were appearing in increasing numbers. This led to apprehension that the proficiency level of the Wing would decline, because of insufficient total experience or at least the lack of recent experience. Extra steps were therefore taken to prevent flying safety hazards from developing. The standardization division was instructed to make frequent visits to the squadrons and to fly frequent spot checks.[53/] The Operational Hazard Report (OHR) program was pressed, and the principle that no load was worth the loss of an aircraft was emphasized.[54/]

Contributing to the shortage of engineers was the gap between the Date Eligible for Return from Overseas (DEROS) of one man and the arrival date of his replacement. This was partially due to the fact that graduation from training at Hurlburt Field, Fla., did not occur until the month of the man's programmed arrival time in SEA. Other factors were the backlog of students awaiting entry into the Clark Air Base Jungle Survival School, and the difficulty of getting transportation from Clark AB to Vietnam. Together, these factors often resulted in a man leaving Vietnam before the arrival of his replacement.

At one time, the situation became so desperate that the Wing asked that a special flight be set up to bring the engineers over to the theater from Hurlburt and that the Jungle Survival School be waived for the engineers.[55/] Though these measures were disapproved for the engineers, some pilots were allowed to skip the Survival School during the spring of 1968; some of the herbicide pilots were used in the airlift role; and some C-47 pilots from within the theater were transferred to

UNCLASSIFIED
C-123 PROVIDER
FIGURE 12

the C-123s. These measures helped overcome the pilot shortage but the engineer shortage in the 315th SOW still existed at the close of this reporting period.

Because of the rapid turnover in personnel and because of the type of experience possessed by the people coming into the 315th Special Operations Wing, a thorough and formal training program was required. The emphasis throughout the entire Air Division was placed on safety; it was made clear that very few loads actually were Tactical Emergency or Emergency Resupply materiel, and even then the goods would do the Army little good, if they were involved in an airplane crash while inbound to the station. 56/ In the words of the 7AF Inspector General's report on the 315th SOW dated 26 November 1968: 57/

> "*OPERATIONS: Outstanding*
>
> *The staff was effectively managing all mission activities and insuring that all aircrews maintain the highest possible state of combat readiness. Highly qualified personnel in the Training Division established a PACAF approved ground and flying training course for Phase I, II, and III training of aircrew members. This provided a means for C-123 qualification and upgrading of staff personnel and other crew members assigned without current qualifications in the aircraft...."*

In addition to those measures, the Wing established a policy to prevent, insofar as possible, the use of standardization pilots in an instructor role; it was believed this would be detrimental to the accomplishment of their primary duty. 58/ A training program was also developed to accommodate problems arising from the installation of jet engines on the C-123s. The Wing Standardization Board participated in a conference at Langley Air Force Base which was convened to revise the PACAF Manual 55-123, governing use of the C-123.[59]

When the C-123 Wing moved to Phan Rang, conditions immediately improved from the maintenance point of view because of the greater space and facilities available. At the same time, however, the unit was moving away from its source of cargo which could be--and was-- very detrimental to its efficiency.[60] Colonel Froehlich, formerly the Commander of the 315th SOW, had several suggestions for overcoming that difficulty. First, he suggested that certain MAC traffic for Cam Ranh Bay and Tan Son Nhut be rerouted to Phan Rang, so as to off-load cargo at the C-123 base and eliminate the need for each mission to begin with an empty positioning sortie. He also believed that Phan Rang was close enough to the sea that cargo could effectively be brought over the beach and thus solve the problem of the C-123 base, while at the same time relieving some of the congestion in the large seaports.[61]

An examination of Figure 13 reveals that the Wing seems to have overcome the difficulty and hauled more cargo with about the same number of flying hours as it had while based at Saigon. This diagram shows quite clearly the detrimental effect of the move to Phan Rang, and the response to the Tet Offensive, whereby the temporary addition of the airlift capability of the herbicide squadron to the airlift task enabled the Wing to greatly increase the tonnage hauled. Finally, it illustrates the recovery in the last half of 1968, when the effects of the move to Phan Rang were overcome. This was accomplished by increasing the permissible ACL for these aircraft which were equipped

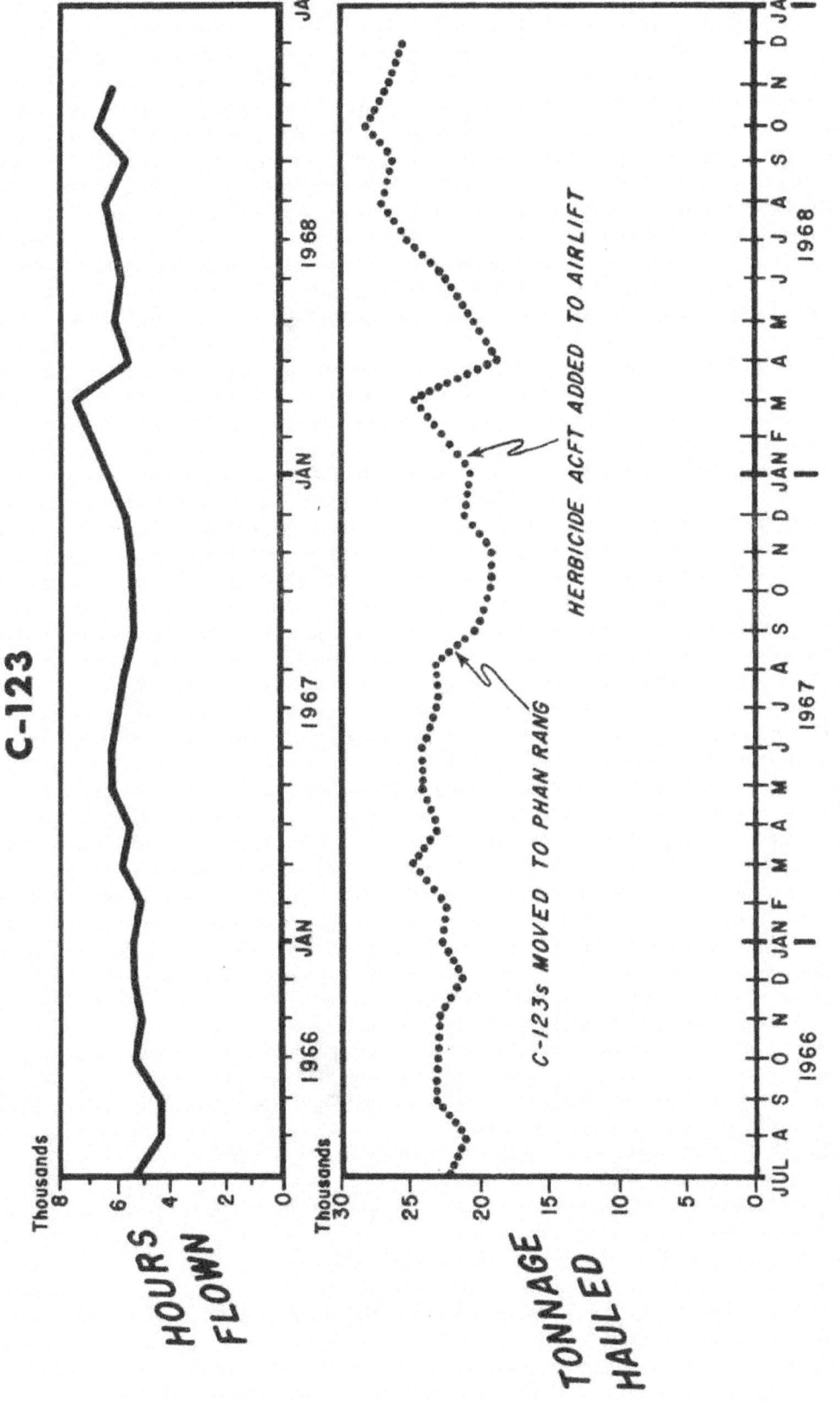

FIGURE 13

with jet engines, [62] by the establishment of more refueling points at forward fields, and by having aircraft on the last leg of the day stop off to pick up the cargo for the next day's first leg. [63] It is probably fair to say, then, that the 315th Special Operations Wing has been both responsive and efficient during the two and one-half years considered, and that it reduced the problems facing the unit to a very considerable degree at the same time.

Although usage of the C-130 in Vietnam entailed certain problems, it is a very excellent aircraft. Like the other transport aircraft in the tactical airlift system in Vietnam, it has a high wing, but it also has four turbo-prop engines and is larger and faster than either the C-123 or C-7. It has carried an average payload of about 7.5 tons per flying hour over the 30-month period under consideration. [64] It is more economical to move freight by C-130 than by C-123 or C-7; however, the latter two aircraft are capable of taking off and landing on a shorter airstrip, therefore servicing more Vietnamese fields than can the C-130. Two problem areas became apparent concerning airlift aircraft during the siege of Khe Sanh: the tires and the wing fuel tanks were too vulnerable to damage in the combat environment. [65]

The 315th Air Division, which was the parent organization of the C-130 force for almost all of this period, was authorized 192 aircraft. Nearly all the time, it had about 200 assigned--though the actual number on hand for use was usually far less than that. To fly these aircraft, the Division usually had enough crew members available to form almost 400 crews. The limiting factor in the matter of crew formation was usually the number of pilots available.[66/] During 1966 and part of 1967, these crew members were assigned TDY to the Vietnam "shuttle" for a period varying from 7 to 15 days. During 1967, it was decided to make the standard shuttle 15 days in length; this figure was raised to 16 days during the summer of 1968.

Some of the in-country commanders were, at first, worried about the proficiency level which would be maintained by crew members involved in shuttle operations. General Momyer, for example, questioned whether such crew members would be sufficiently qualified in drop methods.[67/] General Moore, in his End-of-Tour Report, supported the idea appearing in a study that proficiency of crew members who were continuously exposed to the combat environment would be higher than that of personnel subjected to shuttle operations.[68/] As it turned out, it was the C-130 shuttle crews which did the greater part of the dropping at Khe Sanh and during Operation DELAWARE. As noted earlier, the results were satisfactory. However, the accident rate for in-country C-130s during 1967 was 12.1 accidents per hundred thousand flying hours. That figure was brought down to 5.2 during 1968.[69/]

During the latter half of 1967, PACAF asked the C-130 Wings to state their opinions as to whether the navigator could be eliminated from the flight crews for in-country missions. The Wings equipped with "E" and "B" granted that it might be possible to conduct Visual Meterological Conditions (VMC) operations without a navigator but the 374th Tactical Airlift Wing (TAW) answered that a navigator was required

UNCLASSIFIED
C-130B HERCULES making an ARC LAPES extraction
FIGURE 14

for the operation of the navigation equipment and for traffic avoidance on all flights.[70/] The navigator was therefore retained as a primary crew member.

The facilities for the crew members at Cam Ranh Bay and Tan Son Nhut ranged from unsatisfactory at the beginning of the period to good by the end of 1968. At Tan Son Nhut, the chief problem was security. Crew members were billeted at three hotels offbase and though they were comfortable enough, the 1968 Tet Offensive demonstrated that the whole operation at Tan Son Nhut was very vulnerable in this regard. As cited in Chapter IV, someone decided to bring the C-130 personnel out to the base immediately before the attack, while the C-123 crew members were trapped downtown. Fortunately, there were others in-country who were qualified to fly the C-123; such was not the case with the C-130B unit and had the crew members also been trapped, it would have been necessary to bring in replacements from the Philippines. In fact, during the "second offensive" a considerable number of C-130 crew members in the Merlin Hotel could not get to the base for eight or nine hours. The problem remains and it is a serious one, for all of the enlisted crew members are still billeted in the Merlin, and the entire C-130 operation at Tan Son Nhut can be crippled by a small attack on one building off Plantation Road!

Fatigue can easily become a problem in the Vietnam environment. The mission is such that ten or twelve sorties are often flown in one day. The reporting time changes daily so that part of the missions of a shuttle are flown in the daytime and part at night, thus making it difficult for crew members to adjust their sleeping habits. As many of the missions go into remote fields, where eating facilities do not exist, it is seldom possible to get a reasonable midday meal. The hot weather itself is quite debilitating. This situation has long been recognized and from the beginning, the PACAF miximum crew day of 16 hours was reduced to 12 hours for in-country operations. Still, the aircraft commander had the authority to extend the crew day for one hour and the ALCC had the authority to extend it further than that. During mid-1968, this was recognized as a flying safety hazard, and the authority to extend the crew day was denied the aircraft commanders. The 834th Air Division policy was revised, so that the ALCC could extend it for only one hour and then only for important reasons. This had a beneficial effect, not only in the area of crew fatigue, but also in the area of scheduling. Since the change, the schedule has become much more stable and a crew's progress through the day shift into that of the night has been much more orderly. Moreover, the new reluctance to extend the crew day did not necessarily result in a loss of crew utilization. Since, in any event, the crews rotated back to their home bases on the 16th day, several extensions during the course of their shuttle often resulted in their flying one less mission than would otherwise have been the case.

The operations function at Tan Son Nhut and Cam Ranh Bay was manned partly with PCS personnel and partly with TDY people. The Commander, since August 1967, when the Detachments were transferred from the 315th

Air Division to the 834th, has been a Colonel reporting directly to Division Headquarters. He is assisted by three operations officers, an intelligence specialist, some operations clerks, and administrative personnel, all of whom are permanently assigned to the 834th Air Division. He was further assisted by a number of TDY duty controllers (officers), duty engineers, and duty loadmasters. At Tan Son Nhut, it became impossible to retain the vehicle drivers of the 377th Combat Support Group after the end of 1968, so it became necessary to use some of these highly trained loadmasters as drivers.71/ This was detrimental to their morals. Taken together, Detachments 1, 2, and 3 (Det. 3 was deactivated in Jan 69) of the 834th Air Division constituted a flying unit which was larger than the typical C-130 Wing. Yet, during the fall of 1968, the Inspector General of 7AF had cause to comment that no flying safety officers were assigned.72/ This had a good effect, because the spaces were allowed on the Unit Manning Document, and personnel were assigned to fill them during the following spring.

All transport aircraft under the operational control of the 834th Air Division (except two squadrons of C-7s at Phu Cat and a small detachment of C-123s at Da Nang) are based in the southern third of South Vietnam. This can be very costly when there is intense activity in the north as was the case of the time of the siege of Khe Sanh. Long positioning sorties were necessary and consideration was given to the moving of some C-130s to Da Nang, so as to increase the efficiency of the effort. The idea was favored by the 834th Air Division but rejected by General Momyer, because Da Nang was too vulnerable to attack to allow large numbers of C-130s to remain there for long.[73/] A similar problem arose out of the need for evacuation of Tan Son Nhut, due to enemy attacks during Tet and evacuation of the coastal bases during the typhoons of the succeeding fall. The aircraft were usually bedded down at places where there was no cargo to carry out and thus valuable sorties were lost.[74/]

As mentioned in the foregoing chapter, the step of bringing large numbers of C-130s into the theater on a temporary basis is not one to be taken lightly. Not only is it undesirable to do so because of its impact on TAC's ability to respond to other emergencies, but it also can, and did, cause trouble for both the using command and TAC. When the TAC squadrons came to the Far East, there was no doubt that they were under the operational control of the 315th Air Division except when they were in-country, at which time they came under control of the 834th. Nevertheless, many grey areas existed which had to be better defined. There were many instances pertaining to whether the units would adhere to TAC or PACAF standards which had to be resolved, not to mention the degree to which the TAC maintenance resources would be integrated with those of PACAF. The question finally had to be raised with PACAF, and it was resolved that TAC personnel and equipment would be fully integrated with the PACAF airlift system and would adhere to PACAF standards, but that careful efforts would be made to maintain the identity of TAC resources, so that they could be quickly returned to the United States when the time came.[75/]

Crew training was also a problem, for it was feared that conditions differed sufficiently in-country (from those to which the TAC crews were accustomed) that steps had to be taken to avoid a degradation of the level of flying safety. Instructors were drawn from PACAF C-130 units which were PCS and assigned temporarily to the TAC units to help with the necessary in-country indoctrination.

Morale in the TAC squadrons started to decline after it became apparent they would be retained longer than the originally planned 90 days. For a time, the tour was raised to 179 days and, since many of the crew members involved had very recently finished serving an in-country tour, they were not at all happy. Finally, the problem was solved when the 90-day tour length was restored in June. This was to be achieved by a sacrifice of the squadron integrity normally demanded by TAC. Two crews and airplanes were to be brought into the theatre from the replacement units in the United States, until the entire force had been replaced. The last of the TAC squadrons went back to the United States during early 1969. Still, without their help, the success of the airlift forces' response to the Tet Offensive would have been in doubt.

The conclusions reached in Chapter I for the airlift system as a whole apply to the C-130 as well. It was responsive, and its efficiency, as demonstrated by the tons per flying hour line in Figure 15, was fairly steady until December 1967. Then the curve shows a decline, due partly to the saturation of facilities by the great number of aircraft in-country at the time, and partly due to inefficiency caused by the great number of emergency requests during the period. From its low at the time of Tet, the Tons Per Flying Hour line started to climb, until it reached the pre-Tet level by early summer. On the other hand, the total tonnage hauled by C-130s as shown in Figure 16, was more or less proportional to the number of aircraft in-country. Thus, in time of crisis, when the level of cargo is rising beyond acceptable limits, the airlift commanders had little choice but to bring in as many C-130s as could be accommodated no matter what the effect would be on efficiency.

As the number of airlift aircraft in-country increased, a tragic incident occurred during August 1967, which focused immediate attention on a long-standing and very serious problem involving the safety of aircrews and aircraft. The danger of being hit by friendly artillery shells was a real concern to airlift crews; nevertheless, the first incident came as a great shock to everyone. An airman who was a witness to the event described the tragedy:[76/]

> "At approximately 0950, mission 432 was hit by a friendly artillery round while on final approach for landing on runway 26. Aircraft was at an altitude of approximately 200 feet and less than 1/4 mile from end of runway. Aircraft appeared to take hit in tail section just short of cargo ramp door. Tail section immediately separated from fuselage, fuselage nose-dived and appeared to fall bottom side up to ground.
>
> "Cause: Lack of coordination between artillery and ATC (Air Traffic Control) facility. Artillery was aware of frequency and call sign of ATC; failed to call air data to ATC. Also, artillery crew failed to observe an aircraft just a few yards from the end of their guns...."

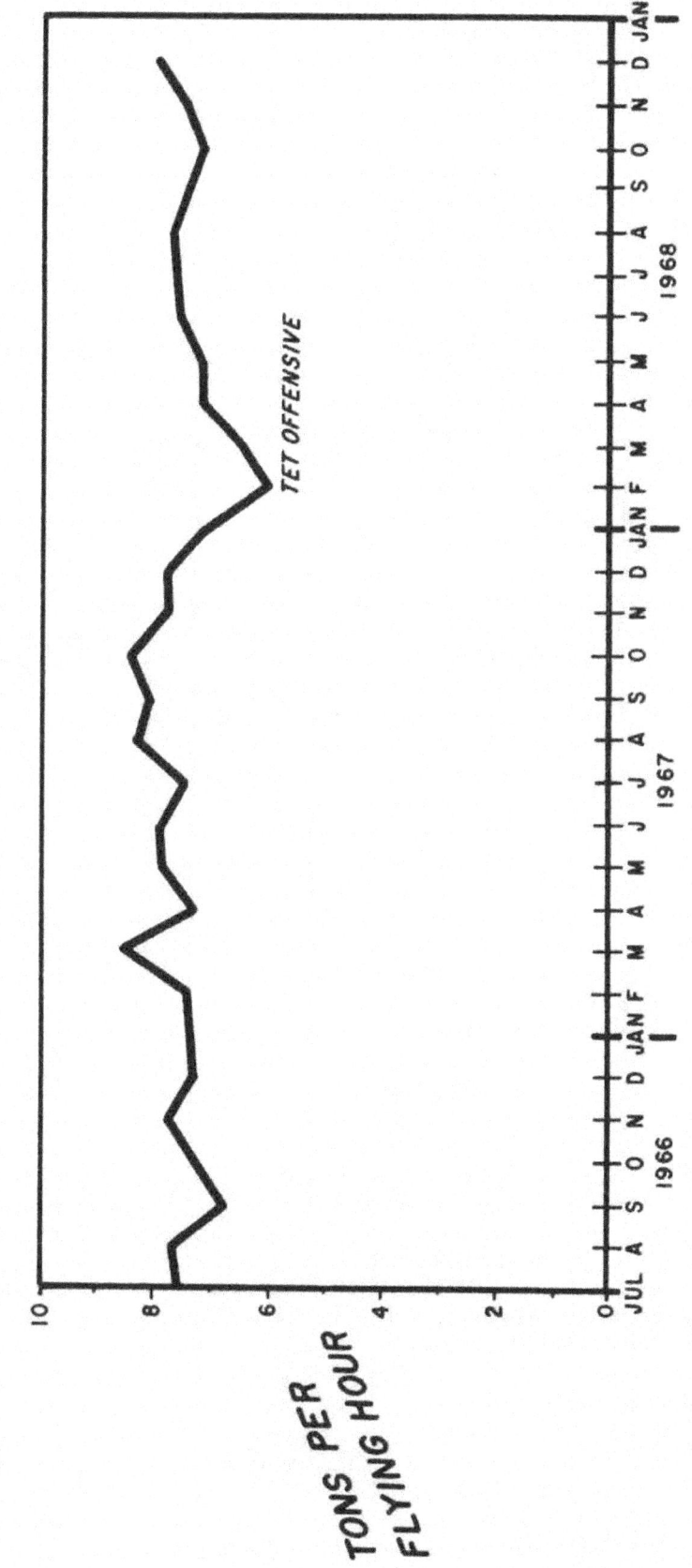

FIGURE 15

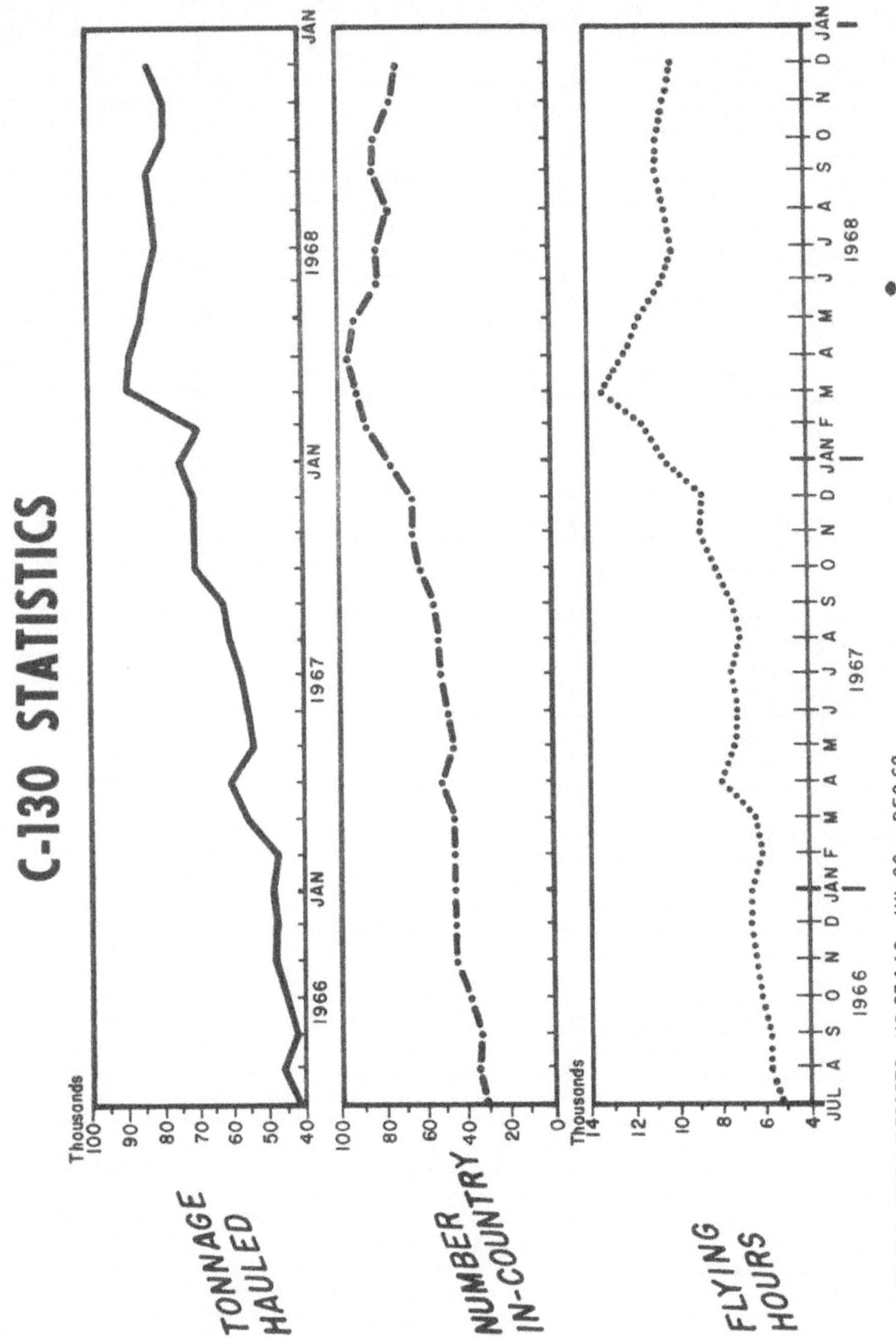

SOURCE: TAPA REPORTS, HQ 834 AD, JUL 66 – DEC 68    FIGURE 16

The airman's account of this incident described the one known case of this war, in which an airlift aircraft was shot down by friendly artillery. However, there was another case involving the loss of an airlift aircraft, in which there was reason to suspect that friendly artillery was a factor.

> *"There is reason to believe that the C-130 which departed Hue on 8 October 67 and subsequently crashed into a mountain, may have deviated from the normally used departure route because of artillery fire."*

Those are the words of Col. John W. Pauly and illustrate again what was, and remains, a very serious problem for the airlift forces in Vietnam: the difficulty of staying out of the way of friendly gunners. 77/

In mid-1967, to describe the artillery warning arrangement as a "system" was to give it a sophistication which it did not possess. In three quarters of Vietnam, warnings were given only for 8-inch and 175-mm firings which constituted only a small part of the whole. 78/ The Republic of Korea forces gave no warning at all. In that quarter of the country around Saigon, warning was not given for any artillery fire that did not rise above 7,000 feet. What warning was given was passed to the provincial Artillery Warning and Control Centers (AWCCs), which were equipped with FM radios. Many of the C-130s were not equipped with permanent FM installations even as late as December 1968. The AWCCs were supposed to pass their information on to the Combat Reporting Centers (CRCs) which could in turn pass it, along with airstrike information, to aircraft. However, the land line communications between the AWCCs and the CRCs were very poor. On a typical flight from Saigon to Binh Thuy (approximately 65 miles) an aircraft commander would contact the CRC at Saigon before takeoff and was more often than not advised that the Dinh Tuong and Vinh Long provinces were "off limits to 14,000 feet". This made it necessary to delay entering these provinces, until it was possible to climb above that altitude with a heavy load, and only then proceed with the 15-minute flight to Binh Thuy. On arrival, it was again time-consuming to spiral down through the 14,000 feet before landing. Thus, because of artillery, the flight was often three or four times as long as it need be. If there were a portable FM set installed in the aircraft, then the navigator could contact the AWCCs for artillery information. In so doing, it was necessary for him to neglect his navigation and traffic clearing duties, while gathering the information and passing it on to the pilots over the interphone system. It was quite often the case with the two provinces in question (as well as many others throughout Vietnam), that there was no firing at all, or that the maximum altitude of firing was something under 5,000 feet. This lack of current information at the CRCs has added great expense to, and decreased the flying safety of, the tactical airlift effort.

Efforts have been made to correct the situation. MACV established the Joint Air Operations Group to study this and other problems. It also has published new directives that require better coordination and sky-watching by the artillery batteries. The 834th Air Division has revised

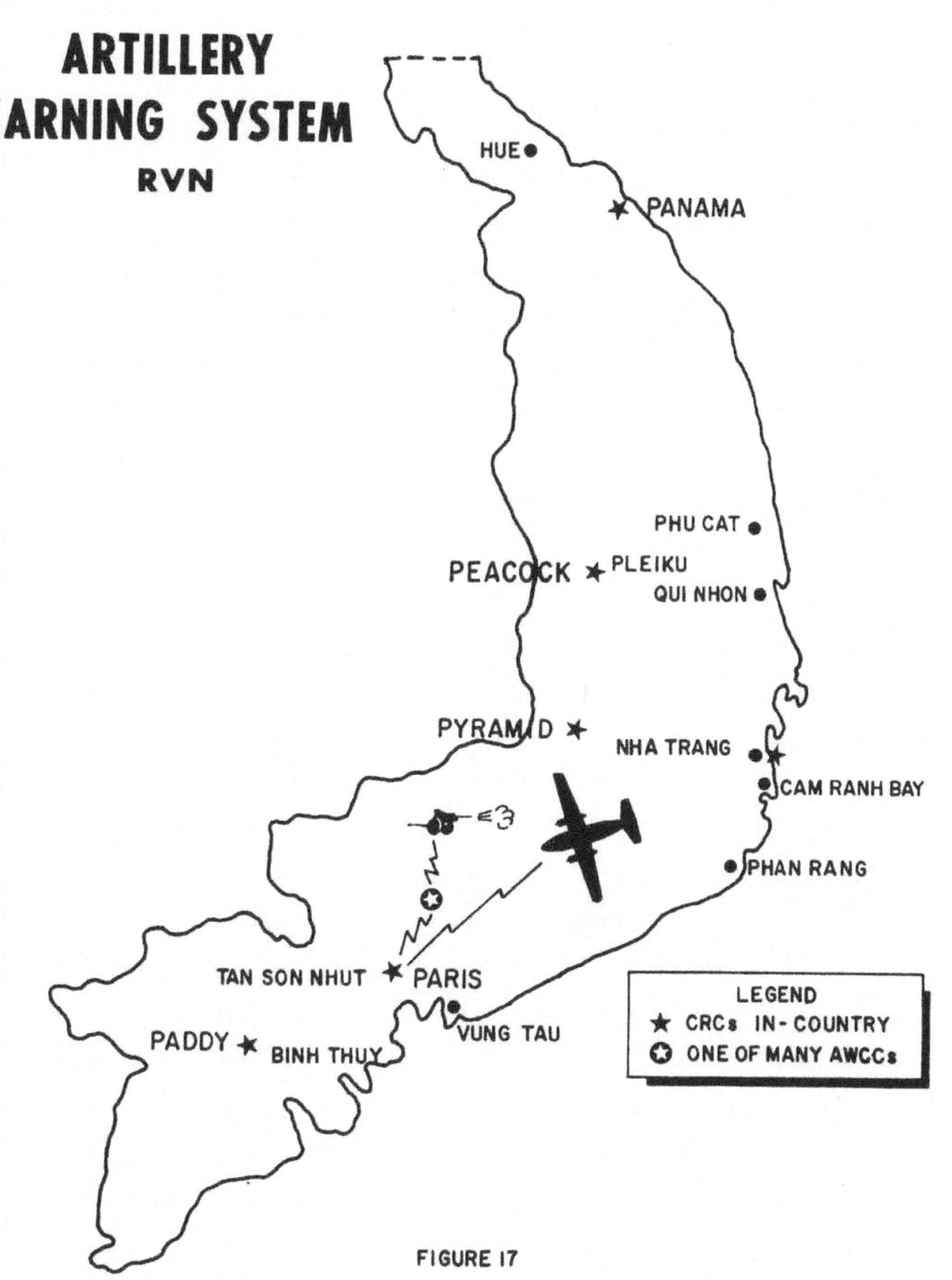

FIGURE 17

directives to its combat control teams and airlift crews, requiring better coordination with artillery units from the former and radar departure procedures from the latter.[79]

At the end of 1968, however, the problem still remained. Though the altitude above which artillery fire was to be reported had been lowered to 5,000 feet, only the heavier caliber fire had to be reported. There was still no centralized artillery warning system; the Artillery Warning and Control Centers were still too numerous for practical use by aircrews; and the communications in some of the aircraft were still not compatible with those of the AWCCs.

There were literally thousands of ways aircrews could get into trouble at the forward fields in Vietnam. Though prodigious efforts have been made to cut down on the hazards at these fields, it is nevertheless true that the greater part of the accidents suffered by the airlift forces have occurred at forward fields.[80] Space is usually a critical problem. Since every additional square yard added to the security problems of the airfield commanders, and since the units using the forward fields were often wholly dependent on the air line of communications for their sustenance, conditions tended to become quite crowded. Many of the accidents have involved striking helicopter blades overhanging the runway; uncontrolled pedestrian and vehicle traffic also constituted a continual hazard.[81]

The camouflage on helicopters and airplanes at forward fields makes them difficult to see from above, and the varying type and condition of runway surfaces radically affect the landing ground roll as well as the survivability of the aircraft's tires.[82/] The rapid deterioration of temporary runways under tropical weather conditions;[83/] the use of inexperienced, nonrated Army officers as airfield commanders; and the lack of proper runway markings and lights all constitute obstacles to be overcome.

There are many things which have been done to lessen the hazard. As time passes, many fields were improved through new construction or resurfacing.[84/] Efforts were also made to reduce the wear and tear on runways by placing additional restrictions on operations.[85/] During the winter of 1968-69, the 834th Air Division undertook a program to develop RCR figures (an index of runway surface friction) for all of the fields in Vietnam. A vigorous program was implemented during 1968, enabling aircrews to immediately report hazardous conditions to ALCC by radio, so that use of the field could be terminated and immediate repairs effected. Since its activation, the 834th Air Division has maintained an Airfield Survey Program in which all operative fields are thoroughly examined twice a year. Data from this program are used to develop the airfield folders maintained for use of flight crews at their home stations and at some of the ALCEs. They are also the principal inputs to the Tactical Aerodrome Directory which is published in the United States for use of all flying units in Vietnam.

One of the problems entailed in forward field operations is so serious as to require separate treatment. The conflict between fixed-wing and rotary-wing traffic has been one of the principal causes of

Operational Hazard Reports.[86/] Not all of the trouble is due to the youth and inexperience of some of the Army helicopter pilots. One of the defenses against ground fire for fixed-wing aircraft is to descend as rapidly as possible and to vary the landing pattern as much as possible from landing to landing. On takeoff, because of ground fire, it is desirable to climb as rapidly as possible and to avoid flying on the runway heading for any appreciable length of time. The helicopter, on the other hand, is so maneuverable that there is no compelling need for the crews to fly a consistent traffic pattern, which would make it more vulnerable to ground fire. Added to that, the Army was suffering a shortage of trained controllers throughout the period of this report, and it was sometimes necessary to place an inexperienced man with only advisory authority at certain locations. At other locations, it was sometimes not even possible to have a man to monitor the radios. Even under the best of conditions, the controlling agency had to guide the fixed-wing craft on a UHF frequency, while it moved the helicopters using FM radios.[87/]

Lately there have been several steps taken to overcome this trouble. Traffic patterns for both fixed-wing and helicopter aircraft have been published in the Tactical Aerodrome Directory and in the airfield folders. The aircrews have continually been directed to see and be seen, and the fixed-wing crews have been directed to fly straight ahead after takeoff until reaching 1,000 feet, and to maintain at least 700 feet until established on final approach. A joint U.S. Army

Vietnam (USARV)-834th Air Division committee was formed to consider the problem, and it was recommended that this committee be elevated to the MACV 7AF level.[88/] This was achieved when the Joint Air Operations Group was created; membership was drawn from all of the Armed Services conducting air operations in Vietnam. This Group and its predecessor have been responsible for many of these steps and have also taken measures to improve communications. Standard forward field frequencies have been published and the Army, which changes assigned frequencies very often for security reasons, has been urged to make more timely efforts to pass this information on to the Air Force.[89/]

Many of the accidents at forward fields have been charged to pilot error during assault landings. Several steps were taken to lessen the chances for such accidents. For example, the Standardization Board of the 463d Tactical Airlift Wing recently published a multi-paged discussion of factors bearing upon assault landings. Included were recommended techniques and briefing items which should be covered prior to landing. As mentioned here, the 834th has developed a program to better define the RCR values for runways in use, and it was emphasized to all the pilots in the command that none would be criticized for aborting a mission which he felt to be beyond his own capabilities. From the very beginning of the period, an extensive orientation program was conducted to insure a high level of proficiency for all aircraft commanders at the time of their initial checkout. An "in-country check" was required of all of them and during mid-1968, 834th Air

Division enforced PACAF policy, so that pilots with "normal" ratings would not be scheduled to fly shuttles as aircraft commanders. Rather, all of them would be required to attain the "assault" or "short-stop" rating before they could be utilized in Vietnam. The criteria established for in-country operations had been such that a "normal" pilot was not permitted to take off, unless he had available a runway as long or longer than the critical field length, while the "assault" and "short-stop" fliers were allowed to go when the runway was at least 500 feet longer than the computed takeoff ground roll. As for landings, the "normal" pilot required the runway to be 1,500 feet longer than the computed ground roll, while 500 feet was sufficient for the others.

Conditions at the forward fields were much improved during the two and a half years which followed July 1966. Many problems remained, however, and Col. Joel Stevenson, the former Commander of Detachment 1, in January 1969, still recommended that more stringent weight limitations for landing on short runways be implemented in spite of the undesirable effect that it would have on efficiency.[90/]

Some attention was given to the matter of aerial delivery methods in Chapter I when the siege of Khe Sanh was being considered. It will be remembered that the Container Delivery System (CDS), the Low Altitude Parachute Extraction System (LAPES), and the Ground Proximity Extraction System (GPES) were discussed, and it was mentioned that a new modification to the LAPES, the "1528", had been developed. The 1528 LAPES is very similar in principle to the older LAPES, except that the flying techniques are a little different, and the newer system makes it possible to deliver loads up to 36,000 pounds on one pass. It had been successfully tested in the United States and also in the Republic of Vietnam during the spring and fall of 1968.[91/] The tests in the spring were on a small scale and delivered 304,000 pounds of materiel to a Special Forces Camp in the northern part of South Vietnam. Those of October and November 1968 were on a larger scale and 25 successful extractions were made at Katum and Thien Ngon.[92/]

The problems in aerial delivery lay not so much in the area of technology, but rather in the matter of policy. The Air Force has long been urging the Army to accept the Aerospace Research Corporation (ARC) LAPES and the later model 1528 LAPES as standard procedures.[93/] The Army, in effect, holds a veto power over the development of all new aerial delivery systems, because it is responsible for the acquisition of the equipment.

Joint Chiefs of Staff Publication 2 states that the Army must acquire all of the delivery equipment which leaves the aircraft. The Army has approved two delivery methods: the CDS and the Heavy Equipment Delivery System. It argues against the development of many aerial delivery systems, because of the great expense involved in maintaining the extra equipment.[94/] It has also stated that it believes survivability of the load is too low for the newer systems, the LAPES loads are too heavy and bulky to permit easy clearance of the drop zone, and the equipment is too bulky to be easily collected and returned to the Air Force.[95/]

The Air Force, on the other hand, argues that it requires a wider choice of tactics to enable it to increase the survivability of its aircraft.

Discussion of the problem has been going on since 1966 and has reached the highest levels of the Armed Forces. In 1966, at the suggestion of Seventh Air Force, MACV stated a limited requirement for ARC LAPES to be used for emergency deliveries, and instructed USARV to investigate the possibility of stating a requirement for more widespread use of the new methods.[96/] Thus, the key to the solution insofar as the Air Force was concerned was the statement of the requirement on the part of USARV; once that was done, procurement through Army channels could begin.

It became apparent that the Army would not soon state the desired requirement, so General Momyer requested the aid of higher headquarters in winning approval of USARV for the new extraction system. The matter was directed to the Chief of Staff of the Army for help. Gen. Creighton W. Abrams, Jr. was the Acting Chief of Staff at the time and his reply was disappointing; he cited the USARV's contention that the new system was not sufficiently reliable.[97/]

At the end of 1967, the Air Force was highly enthusiastic about the 1528 LAPES. MACV could see a limited need for emergency use, but USARV still refused to state a requirement. The Air Force was acquiring the equipment necessary to cover the limited emergency requirement when the siege of Khe Sanh occurred. Soon after, however, Gen. John P.

McConnell, at that time Air Force Chief of Staff, wrote to Gen. John D. Ryan, then Commander of PACAF, and said the procurement program could not go much further on Air Force funds. General McConnell suggested that perhaps another attempt should be made by General Momyer to win a stronger statement from MACV in favor of LAPES; in that way, the approval of USARV might also be won.[98/] General Ryan passed the message to General Momyer who made the desired inquiries of General Westmoreland.[99/] Again the reply was disappointing, for USARV still did not see a need for the 1528 LAPES, and MACV still held to its position requiring only enough LAPES for emergency use.[100/]

There the matter stood at the end of 1968. The Air Force had acquired 100 sets of 1528 LAPES equipment out of its own funds and could win approval for no more. Some successful tests had been conducted in the combat environment, however, and the Army agreed to run a joint test at Fort Bragg, North Carolina, shortly after the first of the year.[101/]

In summary, it is probably fair to say the command and control system constructed to manage the tactical airlift effort in Vietnam has overcome most of its problems. The communications system in use is vastly improved over the one which existed in July 1966; yet, it shows promise of even greater improvement once the SEEK DATA II system and the associated communications equipment become operational. Further, it is also reasonable to state that the Air Force has done a better job of managing the C-7s than the Army did, although it was initially necessary to overman the maintenance organization to bring the fleet up to Air Force standards. (Fig. 14.) In comparison to the other aircraft assigned to the airlift mission in Vietnam, the C-7 is limited by its small weight lifting capacity. During 1967 and 1968, an average of 82.2 possessed C-7s hauled a monthly average of 23,483 tons per month. Their chief contribution has been to add to the responsiveness of the organization. As pointed out earlier, in January 1969, the C-7 could operate out of 40 fields in Vietnam, where neither the C-130 nor the C-123 could be used. The C-123 effort has also been well managed, and the chief remaining problem at the end of 1968 was the fact that Phan Rang Air Base did not generate sufficient cargo to make the initial and final sorties of the day as productive as they might have been. Ever since the summer of 1966, the C-130 operation has also been improving. It has definitely accomplished its mission, although a glance at Figure 15 will reveal the number of tons hauled per flying hour was lower in 1968 than it was in 1967. This is probably not a sign of declining efficiency. It seems more reasonable that the cause was the shock of Tet and the saturation of the facilities arising from far more C-130s being in-country during the latter year than there were in 1967. The artillery warning system in July 1966 was unsatisfactory; in December 1968, the problem had not been overcome in spite of the efforts which had been made to solve it. The hazards at the forward fields had been decreased somewhat between 1966 and 1968, as a result of the many measures taken to reduce them, but many difficulties still remained and the greater part of the accidents suffered during 1968 occurred at forward locations. Finally, by December 1968, the Air Force had developed an accurate, reliable, and safe delivery system in the 1528 LAPES, but was still unable to win approval for its more widespread use.

# CHAPTER III

## MATERIEL PROBLEMS

The C-7s were acquired by the Air Force in January 1967, with many of the personnel who became members of the 483d Tactical Airlift Wing already in Vietnam and attached to the Army's aviation companies well before the changeover date. Accordingly, many of the maintenance problems were anticipated. They were nonetheless difficult--perhaps more so than usual--because of the very poor condition of the aircraft and the differences between Air Force and Army standards of supply and maintenance.[1]

To begin with, maintenance records were incomplete or nonexistent. In many instances it was impossible to determine from the records whether modifications had been accomplished as required to whether time-change items had indeed been changed.[2] Moreover, the Army could not supply the 483d TAW with the appropriate technical publications, and these were not forthcoming from Air Force channels for some months.[3] Many of the time-change items which could be identified as requiring change were long overdue. The Army had not had a corrosion control program and the airplanes were in very poor condition in this respect.[4] Furthermore, the aviation companies did not practice configuration standardization as extensively as the Air Force, so the aircraft came in many different configurations. All of these difficulties, however, could not be laid at the door of the United States Army.

83

The 483d Tactical Airlift Wing was organized with a Consolidated Maintenance Squadron at Cam Ranh Bay to take care of the scheduled and heavier maintenance, while the flying squadrons themselves were to perform the lighter maintenance work. The Wing had to operate under rather primitive conditions for its first few months at Cam Ranh Bay and especially at Phu Cat, which was then under construction (though it has since become one of the best bases in Vietnam). When the two squadrons to be stationed at Phu Cat first moved there, they had to live and work in tents, with use of 3,000-foot laterite runway which, while it was no particular problem for the C-7, did not lengthen the service life of the airplanes. Cam Ranh Bay, by that time, had runway suitable for a Strategic Air Command (SAC) base, but the C-7s were assigned to the east side of the field, which was then in a very primitive state. The greater part of the area was unpaved and this proved to be a tremendous problem, because of the prevailing windy conditions combined with blowing sand. In fact, at first there were insufficient parking places to accommodate all the aircraft and some of the planes had to be parked on a taxiway. The Pierced Steel Planking (PSP) ramp deteriorated rapidly and compounded tire problems. The facilities were especially troublesome, because the C-7 at the time was particularly subject to landing gear difficulties which could be checked only with retraction tests, which in turn had to be performed either inside a hangar, or in wind conditions of less than 10 knots. Since there was no hangar available (except when the C-130 hangar on the other side of

the field was not in use) and, since the wind remained above 10 knots
for days at a time, airplanes were grounded with gear problems for long
periods.[5/] Since the Army had previously established the C-7 operation
at Vung Tau, there were some facilities available there, but conditions
were certainly far from ideal. In fact, the maintenance personnel of
the two squadrons which were stationed there did not have barracks and
had to sleep in a warehouse for several months.[6/]

During the first few months of the operation, there was a shortage
of Aerospace Ground Equipment (AGE), especially light carts. There was
little of this equipment forthcoming from the Army. The shortage of
lighting equipment was particularly damaging, because the C-7 was used
only in daylight operations, which meant that most of the maintenance
had to be done at night.[7/]

Added to those problems was the fact that the Wing did not receive
its full allowance of vehicles until March 1967. Many of those used by
maintenance were not radio equipped, thus causing a waste of supervisory
manpower.[8/]

Training in the 483d Tactical Airlift Wing for the first year or so
proved to be one of its biggest headaches.[9/] Many of the people who
were assigned had no experience on the C-7 (the only C-7s in the Armed
Forces were those in the 483d and the few used for training at Sewart),
and were at lower skill levels than were authorized. Their On-the-Job
Training (OJT) records were in bad condition, and some of these men had
been told that training would be waived in Vietnam.[10/] The very long

hours required of the men and their poor living quarters were not conducive to study and the Wing lacked a good classroom.[11] Moreover, since the 483d was initially activated in-country, and since almost all of the men assigned arrived at nearly the same time, there was a great rotational "hump" each fall which detracted from the continuity of the training program.[12] Combining all of these factors with the press of operations caused the OJT effort to receive less emphasis than it would have in other circumstances.[13]

The most fundamental measure taken to overcome the difficulties inherited from the Army was to overman the 483d, especially in the area of maintenance. In the words of the first Wing Commander:[14]

> "The excess manning in the aircraft maintenance field during the first few months of this year (1967) gave us the essential capability to bring the C-7A fleet up to the Air Force maintenance standards. While improving the fleet's condition, the Wing generated 126% of the programmed flying hours. This additional flying hour generation assured our ability to meet the Army's requirement for retail airlift and exceeded the airlift capability produced by the Army with the C-7A prior to Air Force assumption of control. The decision and actions taken to overman the Wing in the maintenance area were commendable."

Another measure taken to overcome the tremendous backlog of Time Compliance Technical Orders (TCTO) work inherited from the Army was to set up an Inspection and Repair as Necessary (IRAN) program by means of a contract with Philippine Air Lines at the Manila Airport. Some of the configuration standardization work, the installation of the Frequency Modulation (FM) radios, and some corrosion control work was also provided for in the contract.[15] Steps taken to overcome the lack of technical publications included the requisitioning of maintenance technical orders (TOs) through regular Air Force channels, and the participation in a conference on a new flight manual held at the manufacturer's plant in Canada.[16/] The corrosion control problem was also attacked by requesting that a facility be built at Cam Ranh Bay and by programming aircraft through the corrosion control unit at Clark Air Base.[17/] Intense efforts were also undertaken to bring the aircraft records up to date (in some cases it was even necessary to dismantle certain parts to determine whether or not technical changes had been made), and to standardize the configuration of the airplanes, especially the instrument panels.

Of the three methods of improving the primitive facilities available--requesting help through the chain of command to Seventh Air Force, requesting help from the base Civil Engineers at Cam Ranh Bay and Phu Cat and from the Army at Vung Tau, and through Self-Help--only the last was fully under the control of the 483d TAW. A hangar was repeatedly requested and it was approved, but the press of events prevented its immediate construction.[18/] A corrosion control facility was also promised to the Wing and the problem of blowing sand was overcome somewhat in the spring of 1967 by the stabilization of the soil in the C-7 area at Cam Ranh Bay and then covering it with asphalt.[19/] The motor vehicle problem was overcome early, but the trouble with the aircraft landing gear system was more difficult. A request was sent to Air Force Logistics Command (AFLC) for help in reducing the number of malfunctions that were being experienced. AFLC suggested that a special boot be devised to protect the landing gear capsule from dirt and sand.[20] This suggestion was implemented and the problem solved.[21]

The Specialty Knowledge Test (SKT) scores for the maintenance men were far below acceptable levels in the 483d. To correct this deficiency, group study programs were instituted and pre-tests were developed.[22] Additional improvements were made by air-conditioning the training area through the Self-Help program.[23]

In general, the solutions devised to overcome the problems of activating a wing in the combat theater were effective. Figure 18 shows that the Operationally Ready rate was quickly brought above the minimum PACAF standard of 71 percent, and it has been maintained solidly above that level ever since. The number of flying hours for the 483d has been climbing steadily ever since the Air Force took over the program. The desired utilization rate has twice been raised, once from 2.5 hours per day to 3.0, and then again from 3.0 to 3.5. The rate of utilization of the same aircraft while under Army control was about 2.5 hours and the Air Force has had fewer airplanes to work with.[24]

Facilities of the unit were improved in many ways in addition to those mentioned here. The corrosion control facility was brought into operation at Cam Ranh Bay during July 1968.[25] By December 1968, the building of a new barracks for the personnel at Vung Tau was underway,[26] a new communications-navigation equipment facility had been completed at Cam Ranh Bay, and an addition to the engine shop at the latter location was under construction.[27] Most of the units of the Wing were subjected to an Inspector General's inspection during the fall of 1968 and the report states that the training program was outstanding.[28]

The Inspector General's report constitutes substantiation for the idea that the 483d has been performing its mission in a more than adequate manner and that it has been improving. It does, however, point to several problems which remain. In nearly all of the Wing's units, the Quality Control sections have been undermanned in terms of numbers and skill levels.[29] The housing of the troops, according to the report, was still substandard, as was the maintenance of publications. In spite of the fact that the 483d had recently acquired a new wash rack, the report complained of an inadequate corrosion control program. The overall rating of the Wing was satisfactory.[30]

The supply problem was no more tractable than the maintenance difficulties faced by the C-7 organization. In fact, since the greater part of the maintenance function was under the direct command of the Wing, while the supply function was handled by units outside the 483d chain of command, the latter might therefore be termed a more frustrating problem.

One of the most serious obstacles arose because nearly all of the parts of the C-7 were, in the beginning, not standard in the Air Force supply system. Moreover, the C-7s were so far from being standardized and the Army supply records so incomplete that the Air Force supply planning problem was further complicated.[31] The central supply source for the fleet was at Cam Ranh Bay, and it depended upon a computer for its entire operation. Because the Univac computer experienced much down time, it greatly delayed deliveries of needed parts to the Consolidated Maintenance Squadron and to the flying quadrons.[32/] Though one C-7 mission a day was devoted to shuttling between the main base at Cam Ranh Bay and the other locations at Phu Cat and Vung Tau, the geographic separation of the subordinate units from the central source of supply nevertheless led to delays.[33/]

Some of the items of supply which were particularly troublesome were propellers, flight instruments, avionics, engine parts, TACAN modification program parts, and especially fuel quantity indicators.[34/] Since the supply data received from the Army was so inadequate, it was also very difficult to maintain proper levels of bench stock at the forward locations.[35/]

As mentioned previously, many personnel of the initial cadre arrived in-country before activation of the Wing, to plan for an orderly transition. Special efforts were made to identify existing supply shortages to anticipate future shortages. Steps were also taken to build up adequate levels of engines and propellers, as well as many other items, long before 1 January 1967. Permission was obtained for personnel from the 483d to enter the base supply warehouses at Cam Ranh Bay and to seek out those parts which had not yet been entered on supply records. Much time was spent on this task, and the results were helpful. During the summer of 1967, for example, Wing personnel spent an average of 34 man hours per day in the warehouse seeking out back-ordered parts. It was found that more than 50 percent of them were indeed on hand in the storage areas.[36/] In September 1967, a Weapons Systems Support Liaison Officer from the Warner Robins Air Materiel Area (WRAMA), Georgia, was assigned to the Wing in the hope that the solution to the C-7 supply problem could be found more quickly through better liaison with AFLC. During the last quarter of 1968, an interesting solution to a number of supply problems was found. Someone discovered C-7 parts in the Army's Saigon depot valued at $341,201.28; they were transferred to the Air Force without charge, and the supply system of the 483d received a considerable boost.[37/]

The upper curve in Figure 18, which may be taken as a rough indication of supply responsiveness, shows that the NORS rate for the first year of C-7 operations was unsatisfactory; it was often above the PACAF standard of five percent. The situation improved considerably during 1968, but some annoying problems remained. According to the report of the 7AF Inspector General resulting from an inspection made during the fall of 1968, the supply discipline in many of the units of the 483d was not as good as it should have been. The chief criticisms were the failure to maintain a proper level of bench stock in the subordinate units, and the failure to properly document the cannibalization of parts from crashed aircraft. These discrepancies could lead to inaccuracies in the collection of data and, in turn, adversely affect supply planning at higher levels. The excessive amount of bench stock could also lead to the maintenance of unduly high inventories of parts.[38/] The report of the Inspector General added that the relationship between the Army and the 483d units at Vung Tau in the materiel area was not sufficiently defined in existing directives. The C-7 squadrons were receiving some of their supplies from the Army and some from Tan Son Nhut AB; on some occasions, the identical items had come to the units through both channels.[39/] In spite of those discrepancies and despite the slow start of the supply support system of the C-7 organization, it is reasonable to say that it was operating in a satisfactory way by the end of 1968.

The materiel problems of the 315th Special Operations Wing at Phan Rang were similar in many respects to those of the 483d Tactical Airlift Wing. The 315th, like the 483d, had difficulties with its training program which arose from the great turnover rate and the low skill level of many of its incoming personnel; it had its difficulties with supply support and supply discipline; it had obstacles to overcome in the area of facilities; and there were also troubles arising from the introduction of new equipment to the Air Force system--the jet engines on the C-123K.[40/]

During July 1966, the Wing Headquarters, two of its flying squadrons, and its Consolidated Maintenance Squadron were located at Tan Son Nhut Air Base in Saigon. The third flying squadron was based at Nha Trang, and the fourth one was at Da Nang. This split operation led to many supply and maintenance difficulties because it greatly increased the efforts required for good internal communication and supply delivery. Moreover, the units at Tan Son Nhut were greatly hampered by the very crowded conditions at that base; during the summer of 1966 there were 32 aircraft assigned to those two squadrons and they were allotted only

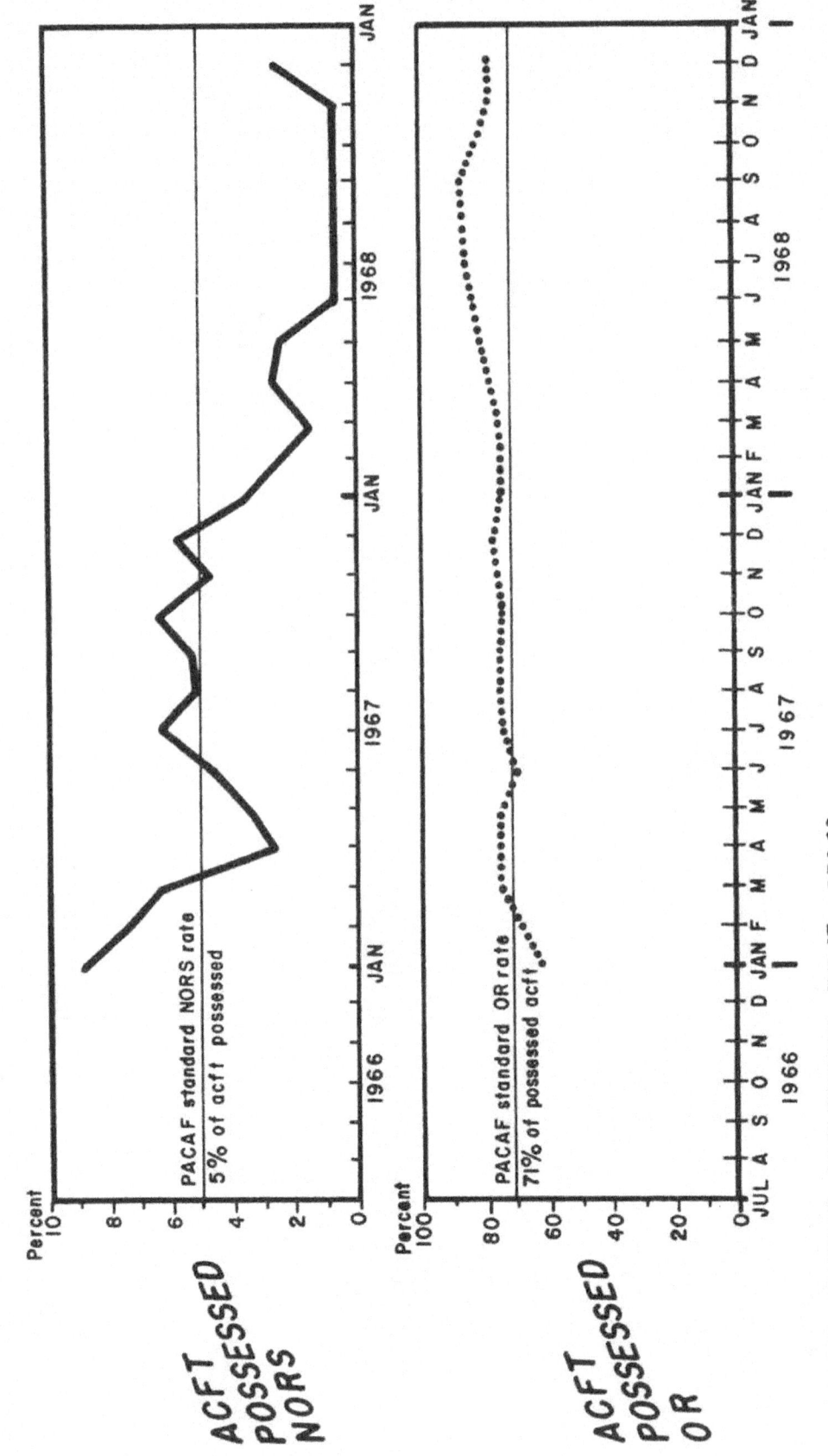

FIGURE 18

19 parking places.[41/] That situation was especially damaging because the C-123 operation was confined to daylight hours, and therefore all airplanes were competing for the available parking spaces at night.

The personnel problem was hardly less troublesome. Just as was the case with the C-7s, most of the Air Force's C-123s were in Southeast Asia and that, combined with the fact that the tour length in the theater was limited to one year, made it inevitable that the experience level of maintenance and supply people would be low. A massive training program was necessary to raise the skill level of these men and to fulfill their OJT requirements. It was also very detrimental to continuity of all maintenance and training programs.[42/]

The former Wing Commander of the 315th commented in his End-of-Tour Report that the decentralized maintenance system was difficult to manage. While it did make for better unit mobility, he believed it would be better for the squadron maintenance officers to be responsible directly to the Wing Director of Maintenance. The maintenance field is now very specialized, and the squadron commanders seldom have much experience in the field. The total maintenance effort of the Wing, according to Colonel Froehlich, could therefore be better managed through the Director of Maintenance. The objection that this would reduce the mobility of the squadrons to an unacceptable degree could be overcome by organizing the maintenance effort into a number of flights equal to the number of flying squadrons.[43/]

A shortage of motor vehicles coupled with poor maintenance was long a problem within the 315th Special Operations Wing. During the fall of

1967, an Inspector General's report on the 19th Air Commando Squadron at Tan Son Nhut cited the maintenance vehicle fleet as being in extremely poor condition. The situation was no better at the parent Wing's location. During the first quarter of 1968, there was a shortage of nine vehicles assigned to the Wing, and this was especially damaging because of the long distance from the C-123 facilities to the rest of the base installations. At the same time, only two of the 16 base buses were in operating condition.44/

Additional maintenance problems arose from the modification of the Wing's C-123Bs into the C-123K configuration by the addition of jet engines (among other things). The program quickly fell behind and the first aircraft was not delivered until April 1967. The modifications were supposed to have been done earlier, but by December 1968 the completion date had slipped to May 1969.45/ Since the jets came to be used much more than had been anticipated added to the problems of maintenance and supply.46/

Though some temporary difficulties were involved, the move to Phan Rang during the late summer of 1967 did much to improve the facilities available for the maintenance effort. The rule forbidding the PCS transfer of in-country men when they had less than 90 days remaining before rotation deprived the Wing of the services of some of its most experienced maintenance personnel during the critical early days.47/ However, the large amount of ramp space and the uncrowded facilities available at the new base had a very beneficial effect on the maintenance effort.

The support received from base facilities improved significantly, and the mission reliability of the C-123 fleet improved from 80 to 90 percent in the space of a few weeks.[48/]

As pointed out, the Wing's vehicle problem did not disappear when it moved to Phan Rang. It was necessary to send certain Wing personnel to the base motor vehicle shops to help with the maintenance of the trucks, so as to get enough of them on the road to enable the unit to accomplish its mission. The problem was also attacked by doing a considerable amount of maintenance on the vehicles in the C-123 area, and by establishing centralized control of the vehicle fleet in the Wing Headquarters.[49/]

The results of these measures seem to have been beneficial. The Inspector General's report of October 1968 cites the maintenance effort of the 315th Special Operations Wing as being very effective, although better quality control was still possible.[50/] An examination of the Operationally Ready curve in Figure 19 reveals that, except for the time between April and December of 1967, the performance of the Wing has been steadily improving. It will be observed that during the last nine months of 1967, while the OR curve was showing a decline, there occurred two significant events which detracted from the effectiveness of maintenance: the move to Phan Rang and the introduction of the K models to the fleet. The jets were used much more than was predicted, and their door actuators caused so much trouble that it was difficult to keep up with the demand.[51/]

In common with the rest of the airlift forces in Vietnam, supply was far from the smallest problem to be faced by the 315th Special Operations

Wing. The chief difficulties lie in imposing supply discipline on the subordinate units and in gaining the proper support from base facilities. At Tan Son Nhut, for example, the Inspector General's report of the fall of 1967 cited the 19th Air Commando Squadron (later changed to Special Operations Squadron) for the careless treatment of aircraft parts. 52/ After a year had passed, another inspection was held, and by this time the situation of the 19th at Saigon was much improved, but in the words of the Inspector General's Report: 53/

> "During the course of the inspection at Phan Rang AB, on three separate occasions and at three separate locations a substantial quantity of aircraft components were uncovered in trash containers and/or abandoned in open storage areas. Most of these components were XB2 or XB3 items, although one item was XD2 coded, subject to DIFM controls. The majority of the items were still packaged in manufacturer's unit packs."

The principal items of supply which were causing difficulty were: spark plugs, carburetors, cylinders, flight instruments, and K model spare parts such as the jet door actuators mentioned before. 54/ On occasion, HF modification kits were ordered and, due to a mix-up at the depot in the United States, they did not arrive for six months. 55/

Referring again to Figure 19, it can be seen from the NORS line that the grounding rate due to the lack of supplies had risen to an unacceptable level during the fall of 1967. During January 1968, an intensive effort was launched to lower the NORS rate and it was quickly brought down to acceptable standards. 56/

Overall, the 315th Special Operations Wing's materiel organization was functioning in an acceptable manner; the NORS rate was good, and all

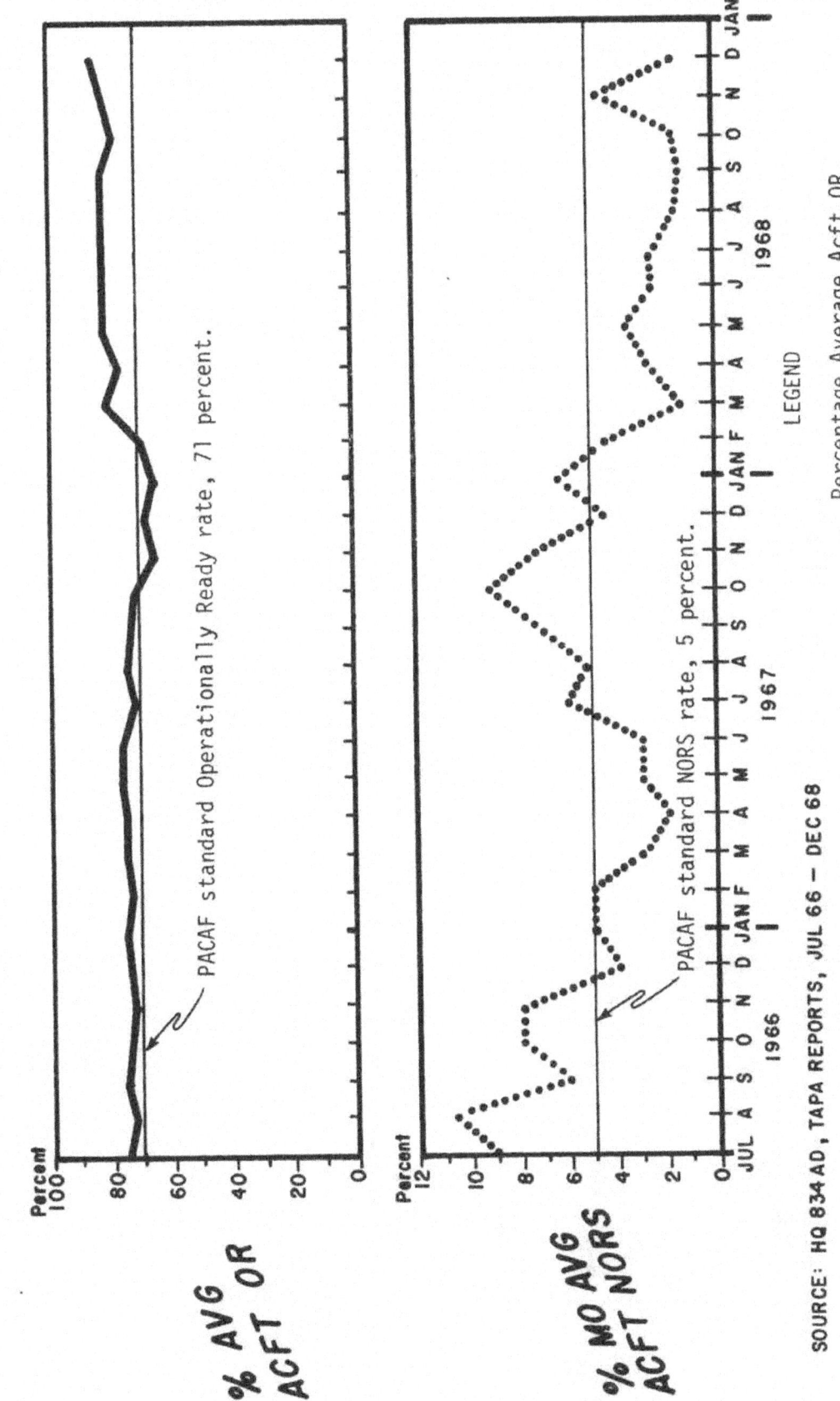

FIGURE 19

through 1968, the Operationally Ready rate was maintained at comfortable levels. The supply discipline problem still existed at the end of 1968, and there was still a shortage of motor vehicles in the 19th Special Operations Squadron at Tan Son Nhut. As stated in the IG report, "The ability of maintenance supervisors to respond to unscheduled maintenance requirements was severely limited by the lack of sufficient expeditor vehicles." [57/]

While the materiel problems of the C-7 and C-123 Wings were very similar in many respects, they differed from those of the C-130 Detachments not only because of a large difference in the sophistication of the vehicle, but also because the whole philosophy of operation differed. As was discussed in Chapter II, the C-130s were not even based in-country, but rather carried out their operations functions there in a TDY capacity and went back to their off-shore bases for their maintenance.[58/] Insofar as in-country maintenance is concerned, then, the job was merely to remove the defective part and replace it with a serviceable one or, if that were not possible, to send the airplane to its home base and get a replacement for it. In more concrete terms, the criteria established stated that if an airplane could not be brought into an operationally ready status in less than 24 hours, it would be sent to its main operating base.[59/] By mid-1967, however, the philosophy was changed, so that 90 percent of the unscheduled maintenance would be accomplished at Tan Son Nhut and Cam Ranh Bay; the balance, along with the scheduled maintenance, would be done at the home bases.[60/]

Perhaps the most vexing problem facing the C-130 in-country commanders has been that of personnel. Just as was the case with the C-123s and the C-7s, there was a chronic shortage in terms of both numbers and skill levels. Added to those troubles was the fact that the greater part of the maintenance effort was carried out by TDY personnel who were usually under the supervision of PCS leaders.[61/] This, in the opinion of the in-country commanders, led to instability and divided loyalties on the part of the TDY work force. By the end of 1968, however, they realized their problems in this respect could not be solved by stationing a Wing of C-130s in-country. They believed the effort might have been managed more proficiently under the TDY arrangement, provided more PCS supervisors had been assigned to the 834th Detachments at Tan Son Nhut and Cam Ranh Bay (Det. 1 manages work at TSN and Det. 2 is in charge of CRB).[62/] Continual efforts to gain more PCS personnel were made by 834th Air Division leaders and they met with some success; however, the former Commander of Detachment 1 still remarked in his End-of-Tour Report of January 1969 that even though the unit Manning Document (UMD) had been changed to permit a greater number of PCS men, the lack of "head room" at Tan Son Nhut nevertheless prevented the acquisition of these additional people.[63/]

The former commanders of both Detachments, in their End-of-Tour Reports, also cited the low skill level of the TDY personnel, but these men were assigned in such a manner that the less experienced ones were equitably distributed between the in-country and the home base work

98

forces.[64/] One of the areas where this skill problem was especially troublesome was that of quality control. The 1968 Inspector General's Report cited Detachments 1 and 2, as well as many of the C-7 and C-123 units as not having a sufficient number of skilled NCOs in that function. The real problem, according to the report, was that the shortage of 5 and 7 level airmen was an Air Force-wide phenomenon which was not therefore amenable to quick or easy solution.[65/] To further complicate the personnel situation, the C-130 Wings were not manned to in-country standards (100 percent of the UMD), but rather they were maintained at a peacetime level (about 85 percent), even though the greater part of their work was done in Vietnam.[66/]

The facilities problems were scarcely less troublesome than those having to do with personnel. At the beginning, the C-130 operation at Tan Son Nhut was divided between the bomb dump on the north side of the dual runways and "Rebel Ramp", which was located on the south side.[67/] (See Chapter IV.) Later, the bomb dump was abandoned in favor of "Charlie Row", which was also on the south side of the field, but separated from "Rebel Camp" by the civilian passenger terminal area and a very busy taxiway.[68/]

The situation for Detachment 2 at Cam Ranh Bay was much better than for Detachment 1 at Tan Son Nhut. Though the C-130 ramp was separated from the main part of the base, Cam Ranh Bay was built from the ground up by the Armed Forces of the United States, and the layout was therefore much better than the one at Saigon. There was also far less competition for base space and resources at Cam Ranh Bay than was the case at Tan Son Nhut. The latter base was tenanted with a far greater variety of units because of its proximity to MACV headquarters, 7AF headquarters, elements of the Government of Vietnam, the great Army base at Long Binh, and the United States Embassy. That the field was also used by all civilian airline traffic from many different nations passing through the South Vietnamese capital bears mentioning. The base became so crowded on occasion, that aircraft had to wait more than an hour after completion of their runup before gaining access to the runway. Although that was an extreme example, more frequently, it was necessary to wait more than half an hour during the morning. Such delays were frustrating when the average sortie length for C-130s was about 45 minutes, and the same aircraft was sometimes scheduled to fly in and out of Tan Son Nhut three or four times in one day. It was seldom necessary to wait more than one or two minutes to gain access to the runway at Cam Ranh Bay. Nor was it necessary to move the aircraft for loading or the majority of maintenance work being accomplished there. It was required, however, that a flight crew be on duty at all times to perform engine runups when they were required. The facilities at Cam Ranh Bay in early 1966 were capable of supporting only about ten aircraft, but by 1969, nearly fifty were normally operating out of that station. The surge capacity was such that 111 could be accommodated between Cam Ranh Bay and Tan Son Nhut.[69/]

Though the facilities were not split at Cam Ranh Bay, Detachment 2 did have a problem, since it was operating with two models of the C-130 which were radically different. Part of the fleet was composed of C-130Es from the 314th Tactical Airlift Wing at Taiwan, and the other portion was comprised of C-130As from the 374th Tactical Airlift Wing based at Okinawa.

Unreliability of the A model had been a continual source of complaint.70/ The B model was much more compatible with the E model operation because approximately 80 percent of its parts were interchangeable with those of the C-130E. On the other hand, only 20 or 30 percent of the parts of the A model can be used in the E. This, along with the unreliability of the earliest version of the C-130, led the 315th Air Division to propose that its five C-130A squadrons be exchanged for four C-130E squadrons from the Tactical Air Command. Though the move would certainly have improved the capability of the airlift forces in Vietnam, it was rejected because it would have complicated TAC's ability to accomplish its mission.71/ Thus, it was necessary to live with the unreliability of the C-130A, but a plan was devised whereby the impact of the non-interchangeability of parts among the various models of C-130s could be lessened. Since the A model required a separate stock of parts and a separate maintenance structure, it was decided to move the Okinawa C-130As to Tan Son Nhut and change the operating base of the B models to Cam Ranh Bay. In this way, the maintenance and supply functions of the B model operation could be consolidated with those of the C-130E unit, and those of the A model would be no more difficult than they had been before. It was hoped that beneficial economies could thus be realized--though the move was not consummated at the end of 1968 it was planned for the spring of 1969.

One of the most troublesome items in the maintenance of the C-130 in Southeast Asia was the great rate at which tires and brakes were consumed. 72/ General McLaughlin had said that the brakes were requiring replacement at a rate 200 percent greater and the tires 300 percent faster than was the case with the C-130 Wings in the United States. 73/ The ultimate answer, of course, would include such long-range solutions as improving tire and brake technology and building better runways, but several interim steps were taken to reduce the difficulty in Vietnam. Jacks and tires were spotted at various locations about the country, so that the crew would not have to await the arrival of a maintenance team, if they lost a tire at those stations. More stringent standards had been imposed on pre-flight inspections of tires and brakes, in the hope that these measures would reduce the amount of time and effort lost through breakdowns at forward fields.

The Lookheed engineers estimated that the C-130s were wearing out at a rate ten times greater than that which had been predicted, because of the rough usage and short sortie length which were usual in Southeast Asia. 74/ Evidence of this was the appearance of cracks in the wing surface; Lockheed had predicted that this would occur at about 20,000 hours of flying time and most of the C-130Bs now had between 4,000 and 6,000 hours. 75/ The starter control valves, though they were fairly reliable pieces of equipment, were being used at a tremendous rate because of the very short sortie length. The same factor had also caused the wing flaps to be used far more often that was normal.

A massive inspection program was instituted after the first wing cracks were discovered to gather data to revise procurement plans and to devise engineering measures to overcome the trouble. Criteria for a new inspection program were established and when the cracks approached a limit of one inch, the airplane in question was to be grounded until temporary repair had been effected.76/

In May 1968, a program for a permanent repair was approved calling for the entire fleet to pass through the Lockheed factory in Georgia for this purpose.77/ The great usage of wing flaps created a problem which affected both the maintenance and supply organizations. It was found that the jack-screws (large, long worm gears driven by a hydraulic motor and which in turn drive the flaps downward or upward) were wearing out at a rapid rate. This placed a great demand on the supply system, and it was necessary to devise an interim inspection program with increased wear tolerances until redesigned jack-screws became available. The new jack-screws began to come into the system during 1967, and by 1968 the problem had been overcome. The new items proved much more reliable than the old ones.78/ The starter control valve difficulty was largely a problem for supply and was controlled when more of these items were brought into the inventory. Efforts were also made to improve the quality of the valves, but the problem, although not critical, remained.79/

Another difficulty in the supply system was improper documentation of data concerning cannibalization of parts from crashed aircraft, so that erroneous supply planning became inevitable. 80/ During the early part of the period, neither of the C-130 Detachments had the services of a supply officer, but later one was assigned to each. 81/ The airlift organization in Vietnam did not have an organic supply capability; except for built-up engines and props for C-130s, which came from the offshore bases, all supplies were provided by host base supply units.

Though the NORS rates for the C-130s were satisfactory by PACAF standards throughout the year 1968, the commanders involved thought there was room for improvement in the supply support they were receiving from their host bases. Col. Robert Ventres, the former Commander of Detachment 2, in his End-of-Tour Report of 10 October 1968 said that delivery of parts from the base warehouse was not as good as it might have been. He stated that the detachment did not have the transportation to bring the parts over to the west side of the base from the warehouse and that a supply point in the C-130 hangar was needed. 82/ The Commander of Detachment 1, Col. Joel C. Stevenson, in his End-of-Tour Report dated January 1969 said: 83/

> *"Ineffective Supply Support is an item of Command interest. For the seven months preceding December, our NORS rate was 6.1% and we averaged 86 cannibalizations per month. We have asked for the assignment of a W/SSLO and are hopeful of obtaining use of one in the near future."*

The average Operationally Ready rate from December 1967 to December 1968 for the C-130s was 74.8 percent.[84/] This figure was above the Air Force Standard of 71 percent, but it should be remembered that all scheduled and most of the heavy maintenance was done at Naha, Clark, and Taiwan. The NORS rate for the same period was 3.3 percent,[85/] and that, too, was satisfactory with respect to Air Force standards, but again the statement must be qualified, as all of the engines and propellers were supplied by offshore bases and many airplanes with serious maintenance problems were often flown back to those bases for repairs.

In the final analysis, equating that cargo has been moved and the system has proved responsive, the materiel system supporting airlift operations has done the job. At the same time, it is also true that there remains room for improvement in maintenance and supply.

# CHAPTER IV
## AERIAL PORT OPERATIONS IN SOUTHEAST ASIA

There has been a tremendous advance in the technology of air transportation since the Berlin Airlift two decades ago. In those days, the loading and unloading of an aircraft was a torturous process of wrestling coal bags by muscle power into the cargo compartment of a C-54. The loading process has been improved through the creation of the 463L system which makes possible the loading of five or six times as much cargo in perhaps one-tenth of the time onto a much faster and more efficient aircraft. Thus, it is now possible to move far greater amounts of cargo with far less effort and cost than was formerly the case. That is not to say that our system of handling cargo is without its problems. There have been times of crises when cargo handling (because of facilities and equipment limitations) have been the limiting factor on the amount of cargo which could be moved in and out of aerial ports.

In the beginning, the aerial port units were deployed to Vietnam on a temporary basis and remained a part of the 315th Air Division. As explained in Chapter I, lengthening of the war made a more permanent organization desirable. Thus, when the 834th Air Division was activated, the 2d Aerial Port Group was transferred to Tan Son Nhut Air Base in Saigon and became a part of the in-country organization. This group had three subordinate units: the 8th Aerial Port Squadron at Tan Son Nhut with its attached Combat Control Teams; the 14th Aerial Port Squadron at Cam Ranh Bay; and the 15th Aerial Port Squadron at Da Nang. All of these squadrons had numerous detachments at various locations about the Republic

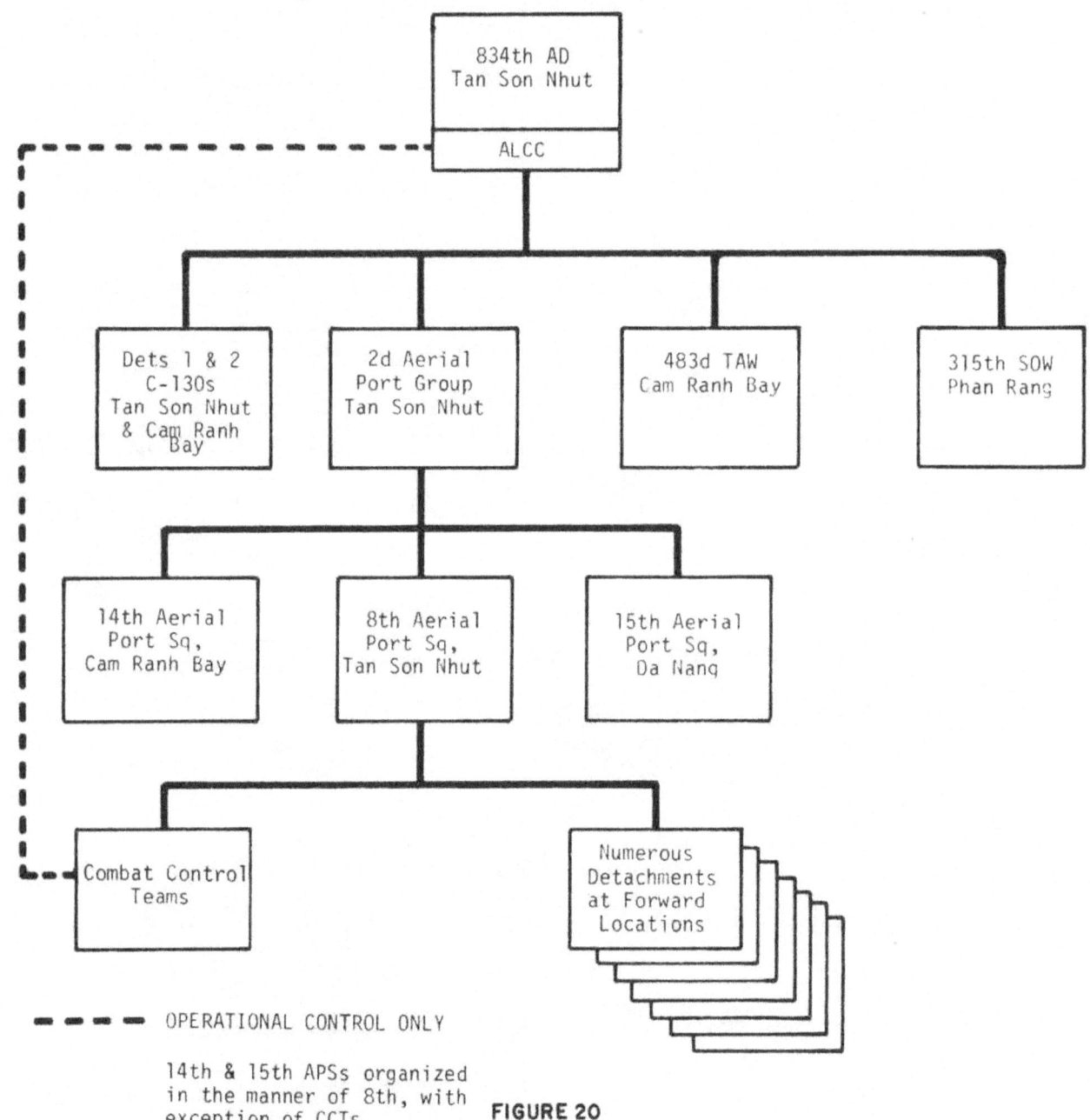

Figure 20

of Vietnam. The organization was fairly straightforward and the problems which were encountered arose from geographic dispersion and the lack of a reliable, dedicated communications net.

As late as 1966, aerial port detachments often found themselves at locations served neither by an ALCE nor a Combat Control Team (CCT). Even when served by such units, their condition was far from ideal, since they had to compete for use of the control units' communications nets. Moreover, even some of the ALCEs had communications facilities which were not always reliable. They more often than not had no radio backup facilities and their land lines were frequently down.[1] Brig. Gen. William G. Moore cited in his End-of-Tour Report that this lack of communications was one of the chief impediments to the development of a truly integrated aerial port system.[2] Often in 1966, an aerial port detachment would know nothing of an inbound aircraft until it was within radio range (less than 30 minutes before landing in the case of the C-130), and sometimes not even until the aircraft was on the ground. This made it almost impossible to plan loads or schedule passengers with reasonably efficiency.[3] Even when a fully operational combat control team was present there were difficulties arising from the type of communications equipment on hand. At Khe Sanh, for example, it was fairly obvious that the enemy was monitoring the frequencies because the timing of his rocket and mortar fire very often coincided with the arrival times of the aircraft.[4] Some improvement was made during 1966 when permission to use the ALCE dedicated lines was won and, later in the year, when a Traffic Management Office (TMO) was established within the ALCC to coordinate matters pertaining to aerial ports.[5/] Construction was going on at a rapid pace throughout Vietnam, and communications of the ALCEs were also improving. Still, as late as February 1967, ten out of eleven ALCEs' backup VHF sets were inoperational and scarcely more than half of the 35 authorized HF sets had actually been installed.[6/] By the end of 1968, most of the work on the command and control nets had been completed, but complaints continued that the aerial port units needed a dedicated and secure system of their own. The efficient operation of an aerial port system required the transmission of vast quantities of data in a secure fashion, but this could not be accomplished using the system extant in December 1968. As was explained in Chapter II, the ideal solution would have been to expand the UYA-7 system to include all of the remotely located aerial port units.

The Second Aerial Port Group experienced personnel problems which were unique in some respects and which were very difficult to solve. Since the requirement for port personnel in the United States was not nearly as intense as it was in Vietnam, many of the incoming personnel were necessarily individuals whose former jobs had little or nothing to do with the duties to which they were assigned in Vietnam. This resulted in a very large proportion of port personnel being in a cross-training OJT status. It also led to an imbalance between skill level and military rank, causing a morale problem arising from the frequent need to place the man with the higher skill level but the lower rank in the supervisory position.[7/] Another problem caused by rapidly expanding port requirements was the difficulty of programming the necessary changes in the UMD sufficiently far in advance. PACAF and the Military Personnel Center have made great efforts to solve this problem but the inherent lag has caused the Aerial Port Group to be continuously short of personnel.[8/] Flexibility, is, of course, a highly desirable characteristic for any military organization. Both General Moore and General McLaughlin have indicated there is a point beyond which the addition of aircraft to the airlift system in Southeast Asia will cause a decline in efficiency.[9/] This is partly due to the limits of the organization's ability to load and unload aircraft. This ability is limited in turn by the facilities, equipment, and personnel available to do the job. Thus, under the present system, it is desirable to maintain a surge capability in terms of personnel, even though it may at times appear that these people do not have enough to do. During the Tet Offensive, for example, it was quickly learned that additional airlift could be brought in faster than the aerial ports could handle them. It was then necessary to call for assistance and this was provided when TDY personnel from the 315th Air Division, and even from the United States, were sent to Vietnam to help the port squadrons with their work.[10/]

Although the 463L cargo handling system is remarkable, it nevertheless has been the cause of perhaps the most troublesome problems in the entire airlift system. It is far easier to handle a bag of coal with modern fork lifts and K-loaders (multiwheeled, low-profile vehicles with a bed containing rollers which can be hydraulically lifted and tilted to exactly mate with the cargo openings of most transport aircraft). However, the bag of coals cannot be moved at all with a machine which will not work. The equipment is sophisticated, but the environment is very poor for machinery. The skill level of many of the maintenance and operating men is not very high.[11/] The combination of these factors has prevented the proper maintenance of the equipment, and the in-commission rate has usually been in the neighbourhood of 65 percent. Extraordinary measures have been taken in an attempt to overcome this problem. On repeated occasions, Air Force Logistics Command teams have been called in to help with the maintenance of the vehicles and their work has been very effective.[12/] However, usually the effect of these visits on the Operationally Ready rates of the equipment had been only temporary. The maintenance responsibility for the Materials Handling Equipment has long been in the hands of the host bases. It has been suggested that the 2d Aerial Port Group assume this responsibility, so as to exert a greater control over its own equipment. This idea was long rejected by the 2d Aerial Port and 7AF backed that position.[13/] However, the Group reversed its policy late in 1968, and has now asked that it be provided with an organic maintenance capability.[14] The introduction of the new adverse terrain fork lift early in 1968 may have eased the problem a bit. Aerial Port men have been very impressed with this new piece of equipment and claim that it is far more rugged than the rough terrain loader, but in late 1968, they warned that the supply of spare parts for the new fork lift needed attention. The adverse terrain forklifts were used under very trying conditions at the A Shau Valley during Operation DELAWARE and the men concerned said that no other piece of equipment could have done the job. The people themselves, incidentally, deserved commendation in that they evacuated the forklifts. The situation was such that C-130s could not be brought in to carry them out, so the mobility team dismantled the equipment to the point where the components were within the weight lifting capacity of the Army helicopters.[15/]

The problem of recovering cargo pallets, nets, tiedown chains, and tiedown devices has been only a little less intractable than that of maintaining the Materials Handling Equipment. To cite just one serious example, during late May 1968, Maj. David R. Mets was Mission Commander at Quang Tri (a Marine helicopter base near the DMZ). He found there were 12 pallets in use as tent floors, one as a bunker top, and six as a driveway to prevent a pickup truck from becoming bogged down in the sand. Not only do pallets make excellent bunker tops and floors, but the tiedown straps and chains make fine tow ropes while the tiedown devices are good substitutes for mallets. Thus, it has been very difficult for the Aerial Port Group to control these items, especially at locations where it has not maintained mobility teams. Extraordinary methods were required to solve this problem and, happily, they have been effective. Of course, all aerial port personnel were instructed to make vigorous efforts to have the material returned, and the aid of crew members was enlisted when a one-for-one exchange program was implemented. A similar exchange policy was instituted by both MAC and the 315th Air Division.[16/] The exchange procedures, while they did have some effect, were not always practical. The places where nearly all of the equipment was lost tended also to be the places where an aircraft was most vulnerable to mortar attack and the

aircraft commanders were sometimes reluctant to increase their exposure
(not to mention slowing down their mission accomplishment) for the sake
of recovering the equipment. Where crew members or others observed large
quantities of equipment, special recovery teams were sent out to retrieve
it. MACV, at the request of the 2d Aerial Port, sent messages to the
various field commanders emphasizing their responsibility in the matter.[17/]
Though these measures of late 1966 and early 1967 may have had some effect
in stemming the ebb tide of equipment, they certainly had not cured the
problem. In February 1967, the 315th Air Division was down to 46 percent
of its authorized pallet supply, and the 834th Air Division was not in much
better condition.[18/] In an effort to further improve the control system, an
agreement between the 834th and the 315th was drawn up during June 1967.
According to the agreement, the repair capability for pallets would be
concentrated at Tachikawa; the 2d Aerial Port Group would ship at least
300 serviceable pallets mer month to the 315th at Clark; and the 315th
would assume the responsibility of maintaining a meticulous accounting of
the movements of pallets and keep all the commands concerned advised as
to their pallet surplus or deficit.[19/] The agreement did not prove to be
a panacea, and by the first of the year further steps had become necessary.
Early in 1968, a campaign was started to educate crew members and port
personnel alike as to their responsibilities in the area of equipment care.
They were warned against three improper procedures: placing of a pallet
on the ground without a block underneath it; blocking a pallet at only
one point (either of those two practices could cause damage); and failing

to require proper documentation of the transfer of pallets. They were also reminded to return the pallets to the repair facility at Tachikawa at the first sign of damage, and thus to prevent further deterioration of the equipment.[20] That was the situation on the eve of Tet--the Communist offensive aggravated the problem to the point that MAC was threatening to use rope for tiedowns and even floor loading. Of course, such expedients would have crippled the Aerial Port Group, because of the great amount of extra labor required to load and unload in that manner, especially since that was at the very time the aerial port personnel shortage was at its most critical stage.[21] By June 1968, the Tet Offensive had long since spent its force, the siege of Khe Sanh had been lifted, and President Lyndon B. Johnson had announced the partial bombing halt. After these events, the level of airlift requirements seemed to decline somewhat, and the measures mentioned here were having their effect. Both the 2d Aerial Port Group and the 315th Air Division were reporting their pallet supply had improved considerably, though there was still a shortage of tiedown straps and chains.

Until the end of 1968, there had always been a shortage of weighing devices in Vietnam. The problem was solved at the larger depots, but it was still capable of causing trouble at the forward fields. For example, during January 1969, a C-130 was at a 3,050-foot strip named Dong Xoai near Saigon. The mission was to participate in an Army unit move by picking up a load there and delivering it to Nha Trang. In such a situation, the accurate determination of load weight is the Army's responsibility, with mobility teams and aircrews having little choice but to accept its word, since there are insufficient portable scales to equip all of the mobility teams. Though many of the C-130s are equipped with an integral weight and balance system, the device was never reliable enough to use and a recent nose gear modification has deprived the computer of a necessary input, thus rendering it useless. On one occasion a pilot was asked if it would be all right to load an 1,800 pound pallet of lumber on the ramp (the ramp limit is 3,500 pounds). The aircraft commander agreed, and on takeoff he noticed the aircraft seemed tail heavy. Upon arrival at Nha Trang the aircraft commander requested the lumber pallet be weighed--it weighed in at 5,330 pounds! In a more critical situation, that great an error could have been disastrous, so an Operational Hazard Report was submitted. The answer to this report stated, among other things, that there were insufficient portable scales to go around to all of the units working in the field. By the end of 1968, however, the situation was much better than it had been in mid-1966. There were no pit scales at all then--not even at the major aerial ports. During 1967, contracts were let for the construction and calibration of nine, 60,000-pound capacity scales. These would make possible the weighing of fully-loaded forklifts and K-loaders which in turn would greatly expedite the operation.[22/] By the end of 1968, six of these pit scales were already in operation and three more were scheduled to come into use by the end of Fiscal Year 1969.[23/]

The pit scales could do little to enhance the safety of operations at the forward fields. To overcome this difficulty, the 834th and the 315th Air Divisions tested a new forklift weighing device. Both organizations were enthusiastic about the new device. The 834th ordered 110 of them, and the 315th asked that 20 percent of its forklift fleet be so equipped.[24/]

The Combat Control Teams in Vietnam have been organized as a part of the Aerial Port system, even though their function is more closely related to command and control and they are under the operational control of ALCC. All of the members of the teams are jump qualified and, in addition, have been trained in the skills of traffic control and radio maintenance. Their functions include: preceding airborne forces to the objective area by means of parachute or airlanding to set up drop zone markings and to control the drops; setting up mobile communications at forward fields and performing the ground control functions normally taken care of by ALCEs as well as traffic control, if there is no other controlling agency present; and relaying information to and from the ALCC to help the operations staff in their flight following and control efforts.

When the 834th Air Division was first organized, there was only one 24-man combat control team assigned to the organization. It was deemed advisable to maintain centralized control over the team; it was therefore stationed at Tan Son Nhut and made a part of the 8th Aerial Port Squadron. In December 1966, the need for more combat control teams was recognized and two more 24-man teams were assigned.[25/] For a time, one 24-man team was stationed with each aerial port squadron, but in April 1967, it was decided to pull the teams back to Saigon from Cam Ranh Bay and Da Nang and to make all of them, a part of the 8th Aerial Port Squadron again.[26/]

The 72 men were organized into 12 six-man teams, and at one time, during Operation JUNCTION CITY in the fall of 1967, 11 out of the 12 teams were deployed.[27/] The teams were usually led by a mission commander who was assigned to the Combat Operations section of the ALCC on a TDY basis. These mission commanders came from the subordinate flying units of the 834th and from the C-130 units belonging to PACAF. They were assigned for a 30-day period, were fully qualified in the theater as aircraft commanders in one of the airplanes involved, and were placed in command of the mobility teams, as well as the combat control teams when they were deployed to forward fields.[28/]

General Moore, in his End-of-Tour Report recommended that pilots be assigned PCS to the 834th Air Division to act as combat control team leaders. (There were some officers assigned to the combat control team, but not enough to be deployed as team leaders in all circumstances; it was not required that they be rated.) He believed this would insure that the leader would have a better understanding of conditions at the operating locations, and it would be easier for him to win the confidence of the pilots with whom he had to work.[29/] At the end of 1968, the situation at times called for deployment of two officers (one mission commander and one combat control team officer) to supervise three airmen in the conduct of drop operations. At some drops held at Dak Seang during June 1968, for example, the combat control team was deployed with three NCOs, a radio jeep, and an equipment trailer. A combat control team officer, who was a rated navigator and had been in the theater for three years, went with them.

The mission commander who was initially deployed was a major; he was fully qualified in the C-130 and was later replaced with a lieutenant colonel with the same pilot qualifications. Invariably, the combat control team officer knew far more about the control of traffic, the setting up of drop zones, and the conduct of mobility team operations than either of the pilots. The pilots, on the other hand, knew more about the problems involved in making airdrops with the C-130. General Moore's proposal was to combine the functions of the two.

For a short time after the activation of the 834th Air Division, there was a shortage of combat control team equipment, and the problem was temporarily solved by borrowing some of the resources of the 315th Air Division. A more permanent solution was reached when the two combat control teams arrived PCS with full equipment from TAC. 30/

General Moore saw the need for a portable precision approach aid as a part of combat control team equipment, and a Southeast Asia Operational Requirement (SEAOR) was developed for the acquisition of such equipment. 31/ A light Instrument Landing System (ILS) device was designed and tested; it was scheduled to become part of the inventory during 1969.

Maj. Gen. Burl McLaughlin, who took command of the 834th during the fall of 1967, has suggested that a new combat control vehicle be developed. The weight of this vehicle should be 1,400 pounds or less, so that it may be brought to a site by a UH-1E helicopter. 32/ There were instances of mobility team and combat control team equipment, which was very expensive, being lost or threatened, because it was difficult to evacuate due to weight. The incident with the mobility team at Operation DELAWARE with its new adverse terrain forklifts was already mentioned, and the combat control team lost its jeep at the evacuation of Kham Duc in May 1968.

The lack of suitable facilities was a continual complaint at the aerial ports. A hard, dry work surface added immeasurably to the efficiency of aerial port operations, and the lack of such surfaces was a very important factor in the rapid deterioration of the cargo handling equipment and in the difficulty of its maintenance.[33/] A major construction program was undertaken during November 1966, and the progress in improvement facilities was largely a matter of time and money.

One especially troublesome problem was the split operation at Tan Son Nhut. Upon the activation of the 834th Air Division, the C-130 area was divided into two parts: "Rebel Ramp" and the "bomb dump". Both runways lay between the two areas, and it was necessary to use the former place for minor maintenance and loading and unloading operations. The bomb dump area was used for heavier maintenance, however, the aircraft could not be located there, because the route to the place was circuitous and the road was unpaved. This situation caused a great many loading delays and consumed a considerable amount of crew resources, since the aircraft could not be towed to "Rebel Ramp" for loading but rather had to be taxied.[34/] The problem was, of course, recognized and great efforts were made to solve it. The paved area on "Charlie Row" was expanded, revetments were built there for C-130s and the use of the bomb dump was discontinued in mid-1968. Though the runways were no longer an obstacle between the areas assigned to the 834th, it nevertheless remained a split operation. "Charlie Row" was separated from "Rebel Ramp" and the 8th

Aerial Port Area by the civilian passenger terminal and ramp, as well as by a very busy taxiway. The revetments prevented the towing of aircraft and though the 8th Aerial Port Squadron found it possible to unload terminating aircraft on "Charlie Row", it was necessary to taxi the airplanes to "Rebel Ramp" for loading.[35/] Not only was valuable in-commission time lost in this manner, but it was also deemed necessary to continue to consume four complete aircrews daily, largely for the sake of moving the aircraft.

The 15th Aerial Port Squadron at DaNang has long suffered from a similar, if much less troublesome problem at their location. DaNang Air Base, one of the busiest and most crowded air fields in the world, has two parallel north-south runways. Both sides of the field are occupied by the ramps and facilities of various Marine, Air Force, Vietnamese Air Force, and United States Army units. The area assigned to the 834th Air Division during the fall of 1966 was split in two. The passenger terminal was located at the extreme northeast end of the east ramp while the cargo area, along with the ALCE, was located more than a mile to the south, also on the east ramp. This sometimes led to the need for repositioning; the area was so small, it was sometimes necessary for an in-coming airplane to wait with engines running until an outbound aircraft vacated a spot on the ramp. At other times, the ramp became so crowded that aircraft, fully loaded and fueled, found themselves blocked and had to wait for other aircraft to depart before they could escape from the area. The problem was partially overcome in January 1969, when a new aerial port complex was opened on the west side of the field. The new complex included an adjacent passenger and cargo area, all-new ALCE and port buildings, and a ramp which is far larger than the old one.[26/]

One of the difficulties that led to inefficiency in terms of cargo hauled per flying hour was the lack of facilities that sometimes prevented the location of the aircraft at cargo generation points. Chapter II explained this difficulty with respect to the situation at Phan Rang, where there were airplanes but little cargo. The opposite problem existed at DaNang, where there was cargo but no airplanes. The problem was partially overcome by having the C-130s, many of the C-7s, and some of the C-123s based at major cargo generating points. More often than not, they were used to haul some sort of cargo into DaNang when they were sent there to pick up loads. Still, it would definitely be desirable from the airlift efficiency point of view to have a group of C-130s operating out of DaNang. This idea was proposed by the 834th Air Division. It did not prove feasible, however, partly because there was no room for the beddown of a C-130 unit there, and partly because DaNang was far more vulnerable to attack than were the other bases.[37/] On the whole, the facilities of the 2d Aerial Port Group have been improving at a reasonable pace and this has had a beneficial effect on the efficiency of airlift.

Many new ideas for the handling of cargo have been tried in Vietnam these last few years. One of these was popularly referred to as the "Cow Bird"--a proposal to haul petroleum products to the outlying fields in the internal fuel systems of the C-130. This plan was to replace the procedures of carrying 55-gallon drums on pallets, carrying fuel in specially designed rubber doughnut bladders chained to pallets, and carrying large quantities of fuel in two large bladders in the cargo compartment, along with a special pump which would be chained to the ramp. In the latter procedure, the fuel was pumped through the hoses to bladders already on the ground at forward fields, while in other procedures, the doughnuts and the drums would be discharged from the aircraft along with the fuel. The "Cow Bird" idea was tried in late 1966 and found to be an excellent procedure, because it cut down on the expense of extra equipment, allowed carrying a large load on every sortie, and permitted the hauling of some cargo along with the load of fuel. It was, however, necessary to retain two "bladder birds" on the schedule to service those units using aviation gasoline, for it was believed the use of aviation gasoline in the tanks of the C-130 might prove detrimental from the maintenance standpoint. It was further necessary to continue the use of doughnuts and drums for those users who did not use sufficient fuel to warrant the dispatch of the "bladder" or the "Cow Bird". [38/]

Another promising idea was the substitution of seat pallets for the normally rigged seats in the C-130. The proposal was to manufacture pallets which would fit into the dual rail system of the C-130, and which would have several rows of seats built right into them. Each pallet was to be twice the length of the ordinary 463L pallet and was to accommodate 40 passengers. Two such pallets would be loaded onto the aircraft and the space on the aircraft ramp was to be used for baggage. Such seats would certainly not be as comfortable as the webbed C-130 seats; however, they would surely be more comfortable than the combat loading type and, since the average length of a sortie is only three quarters of an hour in Vietnam, the lack of comfort would be acceptable. The value of the system would be that a considerable amount of delay could be avoided. Without the seat pallets, any important maintenance difficulties encountered during the pre-flight inspection would almost certainly delay take-off. Even if a spare aircraft were available, it was generally impossible to rerig it from the cargo to the passenger configuration in sufficient time to avoid a delay. Were the seat pallets in use, the job of switching aircraft could be accomplished in a matter of minutes. The idea was proposed to PACAF early in 1968 for adoption as a standard piece of equipment but it has not been approved.[39/] PACAF and TAC concurred, however, USAF did not agree that additional support equipment was required for passenger flights in SEA.[40/]

Another simple idea that paid dividents was the development of mail containers. Two types were designed so they would handily fit into the C-130 with its dual rail system, and yet could be delivered directly to the post offices and loaded and unloaded there. This saved the aerial port people the trouble of putting the mail on the pallets, and at the same time made possible the placing of larger amounts of mail on the individual pallet, thus contributing to the efficiency of the entire operation.[41/]

How does one measure the effectiveness of an aerial port? There are no precedents for the scale or the nature of the work in Vietnam, but Air Force doctrine is expicit about the criteria to be used: the first measure of any tactical airlift organization must be responsiveness.[42/]

But beyond that, doctrine and the principles of war alike dictate that the mission must be accomplished with as much economy of force as is possible. The 2d Aerial Port Group had assigned about 1,700 personnel during the latter half of 1966,[43/] and that figure had grown to about 2,500 people during the closing months of 1968.[44/] During the same period, the cargo handled by the Group increased from about 170,000 tons per month to about 280,000 tons.[45/] Thus, while manning was increasing about 47 percent, the cargo being moved increase by approximately 64 percent. That, of course, represents a gain in efficiency and is commendable. Because the Vietnam experience is unique, there are no parameters available to measure the efficiency of the unit; however, the port has kept the cargo moving and there have not been any emergency instances where the Aerial Port Group has failed to deliver the cargo in time to enable the rest of the organization to respond within the established time limits.[46/]

# CHAPTER V
## FUTURE ALTERNATIVES

It remains impossible to predict the exact, or even general, nature of future wars. Whatever our postwar organization, it must above all remain flexible. Responsiveness is sometimes served by a proliferation of weapon systems but that is not the case with efficiency. Since the two goals are often contradictory, it will be very difficult to develop a single organization or a single weapon system which will fulfill both purposes. The experience of Vietnam suggests possible directions of the evolution in tactical airlift in an insurgent environment.

One direction might lead to tactical airlift organizations with two branches; one to serve the needs of responsiveness and the other to serve the needs of mass and speed. This would entail the development of two weapon systems as opposed to the three we have in use in Vietnam or the one which is envisioned by many of the writers on the subject of the Light Intratheater Transport. For the responsiveness branch, an aircraft of rugged construction would be required with takeoff and landing characteristics as good if not better than those of the C-7, and an ACL of at least 16,000 pounds, so as to have the capability of delivering the standard Army two and a half ton truck; additionally, the aircraft should be compatible with the 463L MHE system. The weapon system for the mass and speed branch should have a larger ACL than the C-130, but the wing span should be no greater. Takeoff and landing characteristics should be at least as good as the C-130, with performance assisted by the use of leading edge slats, better engines and props, and laminar flow; costs for these technological sophistications would be offset many times over because of reduced airfield construction and defense costs. Such an aircraft would have an intercontinental capability with a possible capacity for air-to-air refueling, an alternative that might prolong the usefulness of the KC-135.

Another possible evolutionary direction of weapon system development for tactical airlift is the one suggested by General McLaughlin. In his End-of-Tour Report, he calls attention to the excellent and outstanding performance record of the C-130, C-123 and C-7A but stresses that "our greatest immediate need is for a replacement for the aging C-123 Providers and C-7A Caribous".[1/] Such an aircraft should be a sturdy, simple craft with an ACL of at least 10,000 pounds and STOL characteristics as good or better than the C-7; it could be obtained "off-the-shelf" and provide an acceptable follow-on to the C-123 and C-7A.[2/]

Provided with the interim STOL just described, General McLaughlin makes the judgment that the USAF can then "afford to wait for the LIT as the final complement to the strategic airlift of the C-141 and C-5".[3/] Anticipating the delivery of the LIT in the mid-seventies, he provides an interesting description of his image of the characteristics of a single aircraft to replace the three curently in use. Clearly, he envisions in the one aircraft a machine fulfilling the needs of responsiveness as well as the needs of mass and speed:[4/]

> "Air supply of the most rudimentary forward operating bases requires aircraft with a vertical or near vertical operating capability such as present

> helicopters possess. The V/STOL capability would best satisfy this need. It should have enough range to be deployable from the CONUS to all parts of the world, operate from 300-500 foot airstrips in the STOL mode with a 15-ton allowable cabin load (ACL), and have a vertical capability with a seven ton ACL for areas now only accessible by helicopters. In short, the V/STOL should combine the hover and vertical takeoff and landing characteristics of the helicopter, and the approximate speed, radius, and payload capability of our C-130s."

General McLaughlin forcefully adds that "The Air Force should make every attempt to pursue the development of an aircraft to fulfill the vertical requirement, or abdicate as part of USAF's mission, the true response delivery role of tactical airlift." 5/

Whatever evolutionary direction tactical airlift aircraft take in follow-on development, the experience gained in Vietnam will be incorporated into the new vehicles. Only a few C-130s have been shot down in the conflict but in addition to those losses, the force has suffered a considerable reduction of airlift capability because of the vulnerability of the fuel tanks. Less vulnerable, more easily repaired tanks and tires should be developed in any new weapon system.

In support of the airlift mission, the materiel organization has served the requirements of the tactical airlift system in a satisfactory way. The C-130 is a more complicated aircraft than the others and has therefore been more difficult to maintain; any replacement aircraft should be designed with ease of maintenance in mind. Though many difficulties arose from use of the centralized supply system in Vietnam, the economies of such centralization are probably worth the trouble. 6/

## FOOTNOTES*

### FOREWORD

1. (U)   Article, Thomas Kennedy, "Airlift in Southeast Asia," Air University Review, Vol XVI (Jan-Feb 65), pp 73-86. (Hereafter cited: Kennedy Article.)

2. (S)   CHECO Rprt, PACAF, DOTEC, "Assault Airlift Operations," 23 Feb 67. (Hereafter cited: Assault Study.)

### CHAPTER I

1. (S)   Hist Rprt, 483d TAW, 1 Apr-30 Jun 68, pg viii. (Hereafter cited: 483d History, Apr-Jun 68.)

2. (U)   Kennedy Article.

3. (S)   Hist Rprt, 315th ACW, Jan-Sep 67, pg 2. (Hereafter cited: 315th ACW Hist Rprt, Jan-Sep 67.)

4. (S)   Hist Rprt, 315th AD, 1 Jan-31 Dec 66, pg 12. (Hereafter cited: 315AD History, Jan-Dec 66.)

5. (U)   Article, J. S. Butz, "Intratheater Airlift in Vietnam," Air Force, Vol 49, Jul 1966, pp 33-40.

6. (S)   Assault Study, pg 90.

7. (TS)  Extract, Hist Rprt, USMACV, 1966, pg 131. (Hereafter cited: MACV History, 1966, pg 131.) (Extract is SECRET.)

8. (S)   315th AD History, Jan-Dec 66, pg 21.

9. (U)   End-of-Tour Report, Brig Gen William G. Moore, Comdr 834th AD, Oct 66-Nov 67, pg 2. (Hereafter cited: Moore Report.)

10. (S)  315th AD History, Jan-Dec 66, pg 5.

---

\* Supporting Documents were microfilmed for this report.

11. (S)  Hist Rprt, 483d TAW, 1 Jan-31 Mar 67. (Hereafter cited: 483d TAW History, Jan-Mar 67.)

12. (U)  Moore Report, pg 27.

13. (U)  Interview, Col Marion Carruthers, Comdr, 463d TAW, 8 Apr 69. (Hereafter cited: Carruthers Interview.)

14. (S)  Hist Rprt, 315AD, 1 Jan-30 Jun 67, pg 32. (Hereafter cited: 315th AD History, Jan-Jun 67.)

15. (U)  Rprt, Whitaker and Patterson, pg 89.

16. (S)  315th AD History, Jan-Jun 67, pg 13.

17.      Ibid, pg 22.

18. (S)  Hist Rprt, 315th AD, 1 Jan-30 Jun 68, pg xx. (Hereafter cited: 315th AD History, Jan-Jun 68.)

19.      Ibid, pg 17.

20. (S)  Interview, Maj Gen Burl McLaughlin, Comdr, 834th AD, 26 Apr 69. (Hereafter cited: McLaughlin Interview.);
    (S)  Rprts, 834th AD, Tactical Airlift Performance Accomplishments SEA, Jul 66-Dec 68. (Hereafter cited: TAPA Report.)

21. (S)  Hist Rprt, 315th SOW, Jan-Mar 68, pg 11. (Hereafter cited: 315th SOW History, Jan-Mar 68.)

22. (U)  Article, Maj Gen Burl W. McLaughlin, "Khe Sanh: Keeping an Outpost Alive", Air Univ Review, Vol 58, Nov-Dec 68, pp 57-77. (Hereafter cited: McLaughlin Article.)

23. (S)  TAPA Report.

24. (C)  CHECO Rprt, PACAF, DOTEC, "Operation EL PASO", 22 Nov 66, pg iv. (Hereafter cited: EL PASO Study.)

25. (S)  CHECO Rprt, PACAF, DOTEC, "The War in Vietnam, Jul-Dec 67," 29 Nov 68, pg 25. (Hereafter cited: War in Vietnam.)

26. (S)  CHECO Rprt, PACAF, DOTEC, "Operation ATTLEBORO", 14 Apr 67, pg 28. (Hereafter cited: ATTLEBORO Report.)

27. (S)  CHECO Rprt, PACAF, DOTEC, "Operation PAUL REVERE/SAM HOUSTON", 27 Jul 67, pg v. (Hereafter cited: PAUL REVERE Report.)

28.         Ibid.

29.         Ibid, pg 26.

30.         Ibid, pg 25.

31.         Ibid, pg 79.

32. (S)   CHECO Rprt, PACAF, DOTEC, "Operations THAYER/IRVING", 12 May 67, pg 77. (Hereafter cited: THAYER Report.)

33. (S)   483d TAW History, Jan-Mar 67, pg 31.

34. (S)   THAYER Report, pg 78.

35. (S)   CHECO Rprt, PACAF, DOTEC, "Operation JUNCTION CITY", 17 Nov 67, pg 2. (Hereafter cited: JUNCTION CITY.)

36. (S)   War in Vietnam, pp 24-27.

37. (U)   Hist Rprt, 2d APG, 1 Oct-31 Dec 67, pg 19. (Hereafter cited: APG History, Oct-Dec 67.)

38. (S)   Hist Rprt, 315th AD, 1 Jan-30 Jun 68, pg xv. (Hereafter cited: 315th AD History, Jan-Jun 68.)

39. (U)   McLaughlin Article, pg 67.

40. (S)   CHECO Rprt, PACAF, DOTEC, "Khe Sanh, Operation NIAGARA, 22 Jan-31 Mar 68", 13 Sep 68, pg 73. (Hereafter cited: Khe Sanh Report.)

41.         Ibid, pg 76.

42.         Ibid, pg 75.

43. (U)   McLaughlin Article, pg 64.

44.         Ibid, pg 64.

45.         Ibid, pg 64.

46. (S)   315th AD History, Jan-Jun 68, pp 73-75.

47. (U)   McLaughlin Article, pg 67.

48.         Ibid, pg 66.

49.        Ibid, pg 72.

50.        Ibid, pp 71-76.

51.  (S)   Ltr, J-45 Branch, MACV, to Comdr, 7AF, 12 Jan 68.

52.  (S)   Interview with Col William T. Phillips, ALCC Dir, 834th AD, by TSgt B. W. Pollica, Historian, 834th AD, 1 Nov 68. (Hereafter cited: Phillips Interview.)

53.  (S)   315th ACW History, Jan-Mar 68, pg 15.

54.  (S)   CHECO Rprt, PACAF, DOTEC, "Air Response to the Tet Offensive", 12 Aug 68, pg 42. (Hereafter cited: Tet Offensive Report.)

55.  (S)   315th ACW History, Jan-Mar 68, pg 15.

56.        Ibid, pg 16.

57.  (U)   Ltr, Brig Gen Hugh E. Wild, Comdr, 834th AD to Dir of Materiel, 7AF, subj: Ops Summary, 27 Nov 67.

58.  (S)   Tet Offensive Report, pg 49.

59.  (S)   TAPA Report, Jul 68.

60.  (S)   315th AD History, Jan-Jun 68, pg xv.

61.        Ibid.

62.  (S)   TAPA, Jul 68.

63.  (S)   315th SOW History, Jan-Mar 68;
     (S)   Hist Rprt, 315th SOW, 1 Apr-30 Jun 68. (Hereafter cited: 315th SOW History, Apr-Jun 68.)

64.  (U)   History, 2d APG, 1 Jan-31 Mar 68, pg 3. (Hereafter cited: 2d APG History, Jan-Mar 68.)

65.  (S)   Tet Offensive Report, pg 41.

66.  (U)   Minutes, Ad Hoc Steering Committee, MACV, "Minutes of AD HOC Steering Committee", 8 Apr 68. (Hereafter cited: Ad Hoc Minutes.)

67.        Ibid.

68.  (S)   Tet Offensive Report, pg 47.

69. (S) Ltr, DO, 834th AD to Comdr, 834th AD, subj: Construction at Cam Ranh Bay, 23 Jan 68.

70. (S) CHECO Rprt, PACAF, DOTEC, "Operation DELAWARE, 19 Apr-17 May 68", 2 Sep 68, pg 35. (Hereafter cited: DELAWARE Report.)

71. Ibid, pg 37.

72. Ibid, pg 35.

73. (S) 315th SOW History, Apr-Jun 68, pg 21.

74. (S) 315th AD History, Jan-Jun 68, pg 79.

75. (S) DELAWARE Report, pg 41.

76. (S) CHECO Rprt, PACAF, DOTEC, "Kham Duc", 8 Jul 68, Footnote 17. (Hereafter cited: Kham Duc Report.)

77. (U) Ibid; Ltr, Lt Col Dave C. Hearrel, USAF, Comdr, ALCE, 834th AD, Da Nang, subj: Kham Duc Evacuation to ALCC 834th AD, 13 May 68. (Hereafter cited: Hearrel Letter.)

78. (C) Kham Duc Rprt, Doc. 9, Interview, Maj John W. Gallagher, Chief, GCT, Airlift Kham Duc, 17 May 68.

79. (U) Hearrel Letter.

80. (C) Kham Duc Rprt, Doc. 4, Interview, Col James M. Fogle, Dep Dir/ I Corps, DASC and Maj James M. Mead, USMC Liaison Officer, I Corps DASC, 16 May 68. (Hereafter cited: Kham Duc Rprt, Doc. 4.)

81. Hearrel Letter.

82. (C) Kham Duc Rprt, Doc. 13, Interview with Lt Col Joe M. Jackson, Det Comdr, 315th SOW, Da Nang, 18 May 68.

83. (U) Interview, TSgt Morton Freedman, 8th APS, Combat Control Team Leader, Quang Tri AB, 24 May 68.

84. (U) Congressional Record-Senate, U.S. Senate, 16 Jan 69, pp 456-457.

85. (S) TAPA Rprt, May 68.

86. (U) Ltr, Lt Col Robert B. Nelson, USA, Comdr, 2d Bn, 1st Inf Div to Comdr, 834th AD, subj: Letter of Appreciation, 25 May 68.

87. (S)      TAPA Rprt, Jul-Dec 68.

88. (U)      Interview, Capt Gary Mears, Hq 834th AD, 16 Apr 69.

89. (S)      CHECO Rprt, PACAF, DOTEC, "USAF Support of Special Forces in SEA", 10 Mar 69, pp 59-61.

90.          <u>Ibid</u>, pp 68-70.

91. (U)      Interview, Lt Col Lawrence W. Whitney, USA, Chief, J-45 Branch, MACV, 18 Apr 69. (Hereafter cited: Whitney Interview.)

92. (U)      Ltr, Gen William W. Momyer, USAF, Comdr, 7AF to Comdr, 834th AD, subj: Commendation, 28 Apr 68;
    (U)      Ltr, Gen William W. Momyer, USAF, Comdr, 7AF to Comdr, 834th AD, and Others, subj: Well Done, 10 Mar 68;
    (U)      Ltr, Gen W. C. Westmoreland, USA, Comdr, MACV to Comdr, 7AF, subj: Commendation, 25 Apr 68;
    (U)      Article, Harold R. Brown, "The Revolution in Airlift", <u>Air Force</u>, Vol 51, Jun 68, pp 114-118.

## CHAPTER II

1. (U)      AFM 2-4, "Tactical AF Operations--Tac Air Control System", Wash, D.C., DAF, Nov 67. (Hereafter cited: AFM 2-4.)

2. (S)      Phillips Interview.

3. (U)      Ltr, Col Malcom P. Hooker, DO, 834th AD, to Comdr, 834th AD, subj: SEA Passenger Schedule, 28 Dec 67.

4. (U)      Ltr, Col Elmer F. Hauser, USAF, Chief, Airlift Forces Div, Dir/Operations, Hq USAF to Col Hugh E. Wild, Vice Comdr, 834th AD, subj: AF Doctrine, 8 Aug 67;
   (U)      Ltr, Col George W. Kinney, USAF, Hq 834th AD to DO, 834th AD, subj: ALCC, undated.

5. (S)      McLaughlin Interview.

6. (U)      AFM 2-4, pg 14;
   (U)      Memo, Maj Donald R. Hargrove, USAF, Operations Plans Officer, Hq 834th AD, 20 Aug 67.

7. (U)      Moore Rprt, pg 41.

8. (S)     Hist Rprt, 834th AD, 15 Oct 66-30 Jun 67, pp 67-68. (Hereafter cited: 834th AD History.)

9.       Ibid, pg 69.

10. (U)    Ltr, Lt Gen William W. Momyer, Comdr, 7AF to Comdr, 834th AD, subj: Flight Following of Airlift Acft, 23 Sep 67;
    (U)    Ltr, Col Louis P. Lindsay, USAF, Dir/Operations, 834th AD to DOS, 834th AD, subj: Flight Following of Airlift Acft, 7 Sep 67;
    (U)    Msg, 834th AD to 483d TAW, and Others, "Passage of Flight Monitoring Information, 10 Oct 67;
    (U)    Msg, 834th AD to All Subordinate Units, subj: Mandatory Radio Contacts, 8 Oct 67.

11. (U)    McLaughlin Article, pp 65, 76.

12. (U)    Memo, Maj Frank J. Bowman, USAF, Project Officer, 834th AD to Gen William G. Moore, subj: Project SEEK SILENCE, 17 Aug 67.

13. (U)    Hist Rprt, 2d APG, 1 Jul 66-30 Sep 67, pg 21. (Hereafter cited: 2d APG History, Jul 66-Sep 67.);
    (S)    834th AD History, pg 77.

14. (U)    Hist Rprt, 2d APG, 1 Jan-31 Mar 68, pg 12. (Hereafter cited: 2d APG History, Jan-Mar 68.)

15. (S)     McLaughlin Interview.

16. (U)    Draft of Msg, 834th AD to ASD, WPAFB, Ohio, subj: Prototype Mobile ALCE, undated;
    (U)    Article, "Mobile ALCE Given First Test in Combat", Air Force Times, 4 Sep 68.

17. (U)    Moore Rprt, pg 43.

18.       Ibid, pg 43.

19. (S)     Interview, Maj Ronald E. Swanson, Management Control Systems Officer, 834th AD, 23 Apr 69.

20.       Ibid.

21. (C)     Msg, 7AF to CSAF/AFXOPHA, subj: Program for C-130 Airfields in RVN.

22. (S)     834th AD History, pg 57.

23.                Ibid.

24. (U)       Whitney Interview.

25.                Ibid.

26. (U)       Pamphlet, 834th AD, "RVN Airfield Listing", 31 Jan 69. (Hereafter cited: RVN Airfield Listing.)

27. (S)        315th AD History, Jan-Dec 66, pg 5.

28. (C)       End-of-Tour Rprt, Col Paul J. Mascot, Comdr, 483d TAW, 15 Aug 67, pg 6. (Hereafter cited: Mascot Report.)

29. (S)        Hist Rprt, 483d TAW, 1 Jan-31 Mar 67. (Hereafter cited: 483d History, Jan-Mar 67.)

30.                Ibid.

31. (U)       Ltr, Brig Gen Hugh E. Wild, USAF, Comdr, 834th AD to Col Elmer F. Hauser, USAF, Hq USAF (AFXOPFH), undated.

32. (C)       End-of-Tour Rprt, Col William H. Mason, USAF, Comdr, 483d TAW, Oct 67-Oct 68. (Hereafter cited: Mason Report.)

33. (S/AFEO)   Msg, 834th AD to Hq USAF/AFRDQ, subj: C-7 Operations, 10 Jan 68.

34. (S)        Hist Rprt, 483d TAW, 1 Oct-31 Dec 68, pg 3. (Hereafter cited: 483d TAW History, Oct-Dec 68.)

35. (C)       Mason Report.

36. (U)       Rprt, 7AF, "483d TAW C-7A Operations", 31 Oct 68, pg 15. (Hereafter cited: 483d TAW Report.)

37. (S)        Hist Rprt, 483d TAW, 1 Oct 67-31 Dec 67, pg 4. (Hereafter cited: 483d TAW History, Oct-Jan 67.)

38. (S)        483d TAW History, Apr-Jun 68, pg 9.

39. (C)       Mascot Report, pg 6.

40.                Ibid, pg 8.

41.                Ibid, pg 7

42. (U)       Memo, Maj Donald R. Hargrove, USAF, Operations Plans Officer, Hq 834th AD, subj: C-7A Liaison Office, 28 Aug 67.

43. (C)        Mason Report, pg 42.

44. (U)        Msg, COC, MACV to All C-7A Dedicated Users, subj: Airlift Utilization, 4 Oct 67.

45. (U)        RVN Airfield Listing.

46. (U)        Article, Cecil Brownlow, "USAF Presses Advanced Airlift Concepts", Aviation Week and Space Technology, XXXI, 29 Jul 68, pg 72.
    (S)        TAPA Reports, 1967, 1968.

47. (S/AFEO)   Msg, 834th AD to Hq USAF/AFRDQ, subj: C-7 Operations, 10 Jan 68;
    (S)        Ltr, DO, 834th AD to 7AF (DOO), subj: PACAF C-7A Flying Hour Program, 17 Oct 67.

48. (U)        Moore Report, pg 20.

49. (S)        McLaughlin Interview.

50. (S)        TAPA Rprt, Jul 66-Dec 68.

51. (U)        Msg, 7AF to CINCPACAF, "C-123B/K Ferry Crews", 31 Oct 67.

52. (S)        315th SOW History, Jan-Mar 68; 315th SOW History, Apr-Jun 68, pg 4.

53. (U)        Hist Rprt, 315th SOW, Oct-Dec 67, pg 15. (Hereafter cited: 315th ACW History, Oct-Dec 67.)

54. (S)        End-of-Tour Rprt, Col V. W. Froehlich, USAF, Comdr, 315th ACW, 19 Nov 66-12 Aug 67, pg 7. (Hereafter cited: Froehlich Report.)

55. (S)        315th ACW History, Oct-Dec 67, pg 45.

56.            Ibid, pg 15.

57. (U)        Rprt, 7AF IG, 834th AD, 28 Oct-26 Nov 68, pg 12. (Hereafter cited: IG Report 68.)

58. (S)        315th ACW History, Oct-Dec 67, pg 15.

59. (S)        315th ACW History, Jan-Oct 67, pg 29.

60. (C)        Ltr, Brig Gen Hugh E. Wild, USAF, Comdr, 834th AD to DO, 7AF, subj: C-123 Beddown - Da Nang.

61. (S)        Froehlich Report, pg 1.

62. (U)  Interview, Lt Col Jack Maret, USAF, Asst Dir/Operations, 315th SOW, 6 May 69.

63. (U)  Interview, Maj Harold Skipper, USAF, Scheduling Officer-C-123s, Hq 834th AD, 24 Apr 69.

64. (S)  TAPA Rprt, Jul 66-Dec 68.

65. (U)  McLaughlin Article, pg 73.

66. (S)  315th AD History, Jan-Jun 67.

67. (S)  834th AD History, pg 7.

68.      Ibid, pg 135;
    (U)  Msg, 834th AD to Dets 1 and 2, subj: In-Country Aircrew Indoctrination, 15 Oct 67;
    (U)  Ltr, Brig Gen William G. Moore, USAF, Comdr, 834th AD to Dets 1 and 2, subj: Orientation of TDY Crews, 14 Oct 67.

69. (U)  Interview, Maj F. Simanke, USAF, Assistant Flying Safety Officer, 834th AD, 21 Apr 68.

70. (S)  Hist Rprt, 315th AD, 1 Jul-31 Dec 67, pg 57. (Hereafter cited: 315th AD History, Jul-Dec 67.)

71. (U)  End-of-Tour Rprt, Col Joel C. Stevenson, Comdr, Det 1, 834th AD, Jan 68-Jan 69, pg 6. (Hereafter cited: Stevenson Report.)

72. (U)  IG Report 68, pp B1, C2.

73. (S)  Phillips Interview, pg 9.

74. (S)  Tet Offensive, pg 42.

75. (S)  315th AD History, Jan-Jun 68.

76. (U)  Statement, A1C Alvin Barksole, CCT Member, 8th APS, subj: C-7 Accident, 3 Aug 67.

77. (U)  Ltr, Col John W. Pauly, USAF, DCS/Ops, 315th AD to DO, 834th AD, subj: Stan/Eval Tactics Program, 29 Nov 67;
    (U)  Memo, Maj Ronald A. Stimson, USAF, Investigating Officer, 834th AD to Brig Gen Hugh E. Wild, USAF, Comdr, 834th AD, subj: Artillery Threat to FACs, 13 Sep 67.

78. (U)     Memo, Brig Gen Hugh E. Wild, USAF, Vice Comdr, 834th AD, subj: Visit to Lt Gen Edmundson, VCINCPACAF, 7 Sep 67.

79. (U)     Ltr, Col Malcolm P. Hooker, Dir/Ops, 834th AD to DO, 315th AD, subj: Stan/Eval Tactics Program, 8 Dec 67.

(U)     Msg, 834th AD to 834th AD ALCEs and Subor Flying Units, subj: Safeguarding Acft from Ground and Artillery Fire, 1 Sep 67;

(U)     Msg, CG, USARV to COMUSMACV, subj: Flying Safety, 14 Nov 68;

(U)     Rprt, JAOG, subj: Addendum to the Rprt, Artillery Warning Working Group, 4 Dec 68;

(U)     Rprt, Lt Col Martin M. Bretting, Chairman, AWWG, JAOG, MACV, subj: Artillery Warning, 21 Oct 68.

80. (U)     Msg, 7AF to COMUSMACV, subj: Airfield Hazards, 21 Mar 68;

(U)     Ltr, Brig Gen Louis T. Seith, Chief of Staff, 7AF to COMUSMACV, subj: Airfield Upgrading and Maintenance, 15 Jun 68;

(U)     Memo, Maj Robert L. Geasland, Recorder, JAOC, MACV, subj: Minutes of Meeting, 28 Sep 68;

(U)     Msg, CGUSARV to AIG 600, subj: Uncontrolled Helicopter Traffic, 1 Oct 68.

(U)     Ltr, Lt Col Edward C. Buckley, Chief TALO, 834th AD to Subor TALOs, subj: Usage of SVN Common Frequencies, 2 Oct 68;

(U)     Msg, Maj Gen Burl W. McLaughlin, Comdr, 834th AD to CS, 1st Air Cav Div/Camp Evans, RVN, subj: Helipad at Camp Evans, 1 Oct 68;

(U)     Memo, Maj Gen Burl W. McLaughlin, Comdr, 834th AD to Comdr, 7AF, subj: JAOC, 7 Oct 68;

(U)     Memo, Lt Col James R. Pierce, USA, Facilities Officer, JAOG, MACV, subj: Minutes of Meeting, 17 Oct 68;

(U)     Rprt, Maj Robert L. Geasland, Staff Officer, Joint Air Operations Group, MACV, subj: ATC, 20 Oct 68;

(U)     Ltr, Col Alden G. Glauch, DO, 834th AD to all TALOs, subj: ATC, 10 Nov 68;

(U)     Msg, CG, USARV to Subor Field Forces, subj: Airfield Conditions, 11 Nov 68;

(U)     Rprt, Maj Leonard P. Ponte, Staff Officer, JAOG, subj: Minutes of Meeting, 14 Nov 68;

(U)     Memo Lt Col Thomas E. Newton, Chief, Support Ops, 834th AD to DO, 834th AD, subj: Trip Report, undated;

(U)     Staff Summary Sheet, Col Houston N. Tuel, Dir/Ops and Tng, 7AF, subj: Answer to COMUSMACV Msg on Flying Safety, 16 Nov 68;

(U)     Msg, Hq 7AF to Subor Flying Wings, subj: Mid-Air Collision, 18 Nov 68.

(U)     Msg, Hq 7AF to COMUSMACV, subj: Flying Safety, 21 Nov 68.

|   |   |   |
|---|---|---|
| | (U) | Msg, COMUSMACV to 7AF, USARV, and CT, III MAF, subj: Flying Safety, 14 Nov 68; |
| | (U) | Ltr, Brig Gen Leo E. Jones, USA, Chief of Staff, USARV to Subor Flying Units, subj: Airfield Operations, 29 Nov 68; |
| | (U) | Memo, Lt Col John B. Fitch, USA, Recorder, JAOG, MACV, subj: Minutes of Meeting, 4 Dec 68. |
| 81. | (U) | Rprt, Lt Col William K. Redmon, Mission Comdr, 834th AD to Director, ALCC, 28 Sep 67. |
| 82. | (U) | Ltr, Col Louis P. Lindsay, DO, 834th AD to DOL, 834th AD, subj: Runway Inspections at FOBs, 28 Nov 67. |
| 83. | (C) | Msg, COMUSMACV to CG, USARV, subj: Repair of Vo Dat Airfield, 21 Oct 67. |
| 84. | (C/AFEO) | Rprt, 7AF to CSAF/AFXOPHA, subj: Program for C-130 Airfields in RVN, 14 Nov 67. |
| 85. | (U) | Msg, CG, 1st MAW to Subor Flying Units, subj: AM-2 Runways, 28 Oct 67. |
| 86. | (S) | 483d TAW History Report, pg 26. |
| 87. | (U) | Rprt, Lt Col Leland C. Tucker, Mission Comdr, 834th AD to 834th AD, DCO, subj: Operation OREGON, 2 Aug 67. |
| 88. | (S) | 483d History Report, pg 26. |
| 89. | (U) | Op.Cit., Footnote 80. |
| 90. | (U) | Stevenson Report, pg 4. |
| 91. | (S) | 315th AD History, Jan-Jun 68, pg 73. |
| 92. | (U) | Interview, Maj John Sims, Combat Ops Officer, ALCC, 834th AD, 23 Apr 69. |
| 93. | (C) | Study, TAC, "Aerial Delivery Responsibilities", undated. (Hereafter cited: TAC Study.) |
| 94. | (U) | Memo, Capt Courtland R. Braden, TALO, TF OREGON to DO, 834th AD, subj: LAPES/SPADS Evaluation Meeting, 28 Aug 67. |
| 95. | | Ibid. |
| 96. | (C) | TAC Study. |

97. (C)   Ltr, Gen Creighton W. Abrams, USA, Acting Chief of Staff, USA to CSAF, subj: LAPES, 9 Aug 66.

98. (S)   Ltr, Gen J. P. McConnell, CSAF to Comdr-in-Chief, PACAF, subj: Aerial Delivery Methods, 6 Apr 68.

99. (S)   Ltr, Gen John D. Ryan, USAF, Comdr-in-Chief, PACAF to Gen William W. Momyer, Comdr, 7AF, subj: Aerial Delivery Methods, 17 Apr 68.

100. (S)  Staff Summary Sheet, Col Heath Bottomly, Dep Chief of Staff, 7AF, subj: Ltr from Gen Momyer to Gen Abrams, 17 Jun 68.

101. (U)  TAC Test Order 68-321, "Joint Army-AF Test 1528 Low Altitude Parachute Extraction System, Feb 69.

## CHAPTER III

1. (U)   Interview with Lt Col Frederick F. Shriner, Asst Dir/Materiel, 834th AD, by TSgt B. W. Pollica, 9 Sep 68. (Hereafter cited: Shriner Interview.)

2. (S)   834th AD History, pg 33.

3. (S)   483d TAW History, Apr-Jun 67.

4. (U)   Shriner Interview.

5. (S)   483d TAW History, Jan-Mar 67.

6. (S)   483d TAW History, Apr-Jun 67.

7. (S)   483d TAW History, Jan-Mar 67.

8.       Ibid.

9. (U)   Rprt, IG, 7AF, "834th AD, 9-14 Oct 67", 14 Oct 67. (Hereafter cited: IG Report, 67.)

10. (S)  483d TAW History, Apr-Jun 67.

11. (S)  483d TAW History, Jan-Mar 68, pg 6.

12. (S)  483d TAW History, Jul-Sep 67.

13. (C)  Mason Report.

14. (C)  Mascot Report, pg 3.

15. (S)      483d TAW History, Jul-Sep 67;
    (S)      483d TAW History, Oct-Dec 67, pg 17.

16. (S)      483d TAW History, Oct-Dec 67, pg 14.

17.          Ibid, pg 17.

18. (S)      483d TAW History, Jan-Mar 68, pg 24.

19. (S)      483d TAW History, Apr-Jun 67.

20. (S)      483d TAW History, Jan-Mar 67.

21. (U)      Interview, Lt Col William Ulrich, Dir/Materiel, 483d TAW, 5 May 69.

22. (S)      483d TAW History, Jul-Sep 67.

23. (S)      483d TAW History, Apr-Jun 68, pg 35.

24. (U)      Moore Report, pp 17-18.

25. (C)      Mason Report.

26. (S)      483d TAW History, Oct-Dec 68, pg 3.

27. (S)      483d TAW History, Jul-Sep 68, pg 13.

28. (U)      IG Report 68, pg D3.

29.          Ibid.

30.          Ibid, pg D1.

31. (S)      483d TAW History, Jan-Mar 67.

32. (S)      483d TAW History, Apr-Jun 67.

33. (S)      483d TAW History, Jan-Mar 68, pg 22.

34. (S)      483d TAW History, Apr-Jun 68, pg 33;
    (S/AFEO) Rprt, Hq 7AF, "7AF Improvement Plan", Nov 68;
    (S)      483d TAW History, Jul-Sep 68, pg 28.

35. (U)      IG Report 68, pg H3.

36. (S)      483d TAW History, Jul-Sep 67.

| | | |
|---|---|---|
| 37. | (U) | Rprt, Hq 483d TAW to Hq 7AF, subj: Cost Reduction, 10 Dec 68; |
| | (U) | Rprt, Hq 483d TAW to Hq 7AF, subj: Cost Reduction, 25 Nov 68. |
| 38. | (U) | IG Report 68, pp L2, D3, K2. |
| 39. | | <u>Ibid</u>, pg H3. |
| 40. | (U) | Memo, CMSgt Howard T. Pendley, USAF, 834th AD (DMM) to DM, 834th AD (Lt Col Holt), subj: OR/Maintenance Delays-Phan Rang, 5 Aug 67; |
| | (U) | Msg, Hq 834th AD to 315th ACW, subj: FTD Tng, 14 Jan 68; |
| | (U) | RAD, 9-218-(1), 14 May 69. |
| 41. | (S) | Hist Rprt, 315th ACW, 1 Jul 66-31 Dec 66. (Hereafter cited: 315th ACW History, Jul-Dec 66.) |
| 42. | (S) | 315th ACW History, Oct-Dec 67, pg 5; |
| | (U) | IG Report 68, pg L2; |
| | (S) | Froehlich Report, pg 4. |
| | (U) | Msg, 7AF to 3d Combat Support Group and 377th Combat Support Group, subj: Utilization of C-123 Trained Maintenance Personnel, 13 Jan 68. |
| 43. | (S) | Froehlich Report, pg 3. |
| 44. | (S) | 315th ACW History, Jan-Mar 68, pg 40. |
| 45. | | <u>Ibid</u>, pg 31. |
| 46. | (S) | 315th ACW History, Oct-Dec 67, pg 36. |
| 47. | (S) | 315th ACW History, Jan-Sep 67, pg 1. |
| 48. | (S) | 315th ACW History, Oct-Dec 67, pg vii. |
| 49. | (S) | 315th ACW History, Jan-Mar 68, pg 40. |
| 50. | (U) | IG Report 68, pg L1. |
| 51. | (S) | 315th ACW History, Oct-Dec 67, 23. |
| 52. | (U) | IG Report 67, pg E2. |
| 53. | (U) | IG Report 68, pg L3. |
| 54. | (U) | Msg, 315th ACW to 7AF, subj: Maintenance Difficulties, 31 Jan 68. |
| 55. | (S) | 315th ACW History, Jul-Dec 66, pg 10. |

56. (S)   315th ACW History, Oct-Dec 67, pg 36.

57. (U)   IG Report 68, pg N3.

58. (U)   Ltr, Col Barney A. Johnson, Jr., USAF, DM, 834th AD to 7th Air Force (DM), subj: Intra-theater Airlift Deployment/Employment Logistics Policies, 5 May 67.

59. (S)   Hist Rprt (Draft), 834th AD, 1 Jul 67-30 Jun 68. (Hereafter cited: 834th AD History Draft.)

60. (U)   Ltr, Col Barney A. Johnson, Jr., USAF, DM, 834th AD to DOP, 834th AD, subj: Weekly Rprt of the SecDef to the President, 29 Jul 67;
    (U)   Ltr, Col Barney L. Johnson, Jr., USAF, DM, 834th AD to Det 1, 834th AD, subj: Responsibility for C-130 In-Country Maintenance, 15 Aug 67;
    (U)   Ltr, Brig Gen Harmon E. Burns, USAF, DCS/M, 7AF to 834th AD (VC), subj: C-130 Aircraft Supply Support, 15 Sep 67.

61. (U)   Msg, 13AF to DMM, 6200th Materiel Wg, subj: C-130 RVN Maintenance Manning, 4 Dec 67.

62. (U)   Rprt, Col Robert L. Ventres, Comdr, Det 2, 834th AD, subj: End-of-Tour Report, Sep 67-Aug 68, pg 3. (Hereafter cited: Ventres Report.);
    (U)   Stevenson Report, pg 6.

63. (U)   Stevenson Report, pg 6.

64.       <u>Ibid</u>, pg 7.

65. (U)   IG Report 68, pg B2.

66. (S)   315th AD History, Jan-Jun 67, pg 32.

67. (U)   Ltr, Col Raymond O. Roush, USAF, DM 834th AD to MA/DOO 834th AD, subj: February TAPA Impacts, 14 Mar 68;
    (U)   Ltr, Brig Gen William G. Moore, Comdr, 834th AD to DM, 7AF, subj: In-Country C-130 Program, 1 Aug 67.

68. (U)   Shriner Interview.

69. (U)   Staff Summary, Col Ernest E. Biggs, USAF, Director of Operations and Training, 7AF, subj: C-130 Base Loading, 23 Jan 68.

70. (U) Ltr, Brig Gen Burl McLaughlin, USAF, Comdr, 834th AD to 7AF, subj: Delay Rates for C-130s, 23 Dec 67;
    (U) Ltr, Brig Gen Hugh E. Wild, USAF, Comdr, 834th AD to DM, 7AF, subj: Maintenance Difficulties, 27 Nov 67;
    (S) 834th AD History, pg 123;
    (S) 315th AD History, 1 Jan-31 Dec 66, pg 34.

71. (S) 315th AD History, 1 Jan-31 Dec 66, pg 33.

72. (U) Ltr, Col Malcolm P. Hooker, USAF, Director of Operations, 834th AD to DCO, 7AF, subj: C-130 Tire Damage, 17 Dec 67.

73. (S) McLaughlin Interview.

74. (U) Ltr, D. T. Crockett, Jr., Vice President, Lockheed Aircraft Corporation to Depts of Lockheed-Georgia, 19 Sep 67.

75. (U) Ltr, Brig Gen Hugh E. Wild, USAF, Comdr, 834th AD to 7AF, subj: Improving Airfields Utilized by C-130s, 15 Sep 67;
    (S) 834th AD History, pg 24.

76. (S) 315th AD History, Jan-Jun 68, pp 217-219.

77. (U) Ltr, Lt Col C. N. Powell, USAF, Directorate of Maintenance Engineering, Hq USAF to 315th AD, subj: Modification for Improvement of Center Wing Fatigue Endurance of C-130B/E Series Aircraft, 17 May 68.

78. (S) 315th AD History, Jan-Jun 68, pg 223.

79. (U) Ltr, Col Raymond O. Roush, USAF, Director of Materiel, 834th AD to DM, 7AF, subj: Maintenance Realiability, 12 Jun 68.

80. (U) IG Report 68, pg C6.

81. (S) 834th AD History Draft, pg 45.

82. (U) Ventres Report, pg 29.

83. (U) Stevenson Report, pg 12.

84. (S) TAPA Rprt, Dec 67-Dec 68.

85. Ibid.

## CHAPTER IV

1. (U) Ltr, Brig Gen William G. Moore, Jr., USAF, Comdr, 834th AD to DE, 7AF, subj: Urgent Communications Requirements, 14 Jul 67. (Hereafter cited: Logan Interview.)

2. (U) Moore Report, pg 4.

3. (U) History Rprt, 2d APG, 1 Jul 66-30 Sep 67, pg 28. (Hereafter cited: APG History, Jul 66-Sep 67.)

4. (S) Khe Sanh Rprt, pg 77.

5. (U) Moore Report, pg 10.

6. Ibid, pp 39-43.

7. (U) Interview, Col Harry Logan, Vice Commander, 2d APG, 24 Apr 69. (Hereafter cited: Logan Interview.)

8. (U) History Rprt, 2d APG, 1 Apr-30 Jun 68, pg 4. (Hereafter cited: APG History, Apr-Jun 68.)

9. (U) Moore Report, pg 3.
   (U) McLaughlin Article, pg 67.

10. (U) APG History, Jan-Mar 68, pg 8.
    (S) 315th AD History, Jan-Jun 68.

11. (U) Logan Interview.

12. (U) History Rprt, 2d APG, 1 Oct-31 Dec 68, pg 24. (Hereafter cited: APG History, Oct-Dec 68.)

13. (U) APG History, Apr-Jun 68, pg 28.

14. (U) APG History, Oct-Dec 68, pg 25.

15. (U) APG History, Apr-Jun 68, pg 16.

16. (S) 315th AD History, Jan-Dec 66, pg 105.

17. (U) APG History, Jan-Jun 67, pg 15.

18. (S) 315th AD History, Jan-Jun 67, pg 107.

19. Ibid, pg 107.

| | | |
|---|---|---|
| 20. | (S) | 315th AD History, Jan-Jun 68, pg 183. |
| 21. | | <u>Ibid</u>, pg 189. |
| 22. | (U) | APG History, Oct-Dec 67, pg 31. |
| 23. | (U) | APG History, Jul-Sep 68, pg 22. |
| 24. | (S)<br>(S) | McLaughlin Interview.<br>315th AD History, Jan-Jun 67, pg 103. |
| 25. | (U) | APG History, Jul 66-Sep 67, pg 8. |
| 26. | | <u>Ibid</u>, pg 8. |
| 27. | | <u>Ibid</u>, pg 29. |
| 28. | (U) | Ltr, 834th AD to 7AF, subj: Mission Commanders, 5 Jan 68. |
| 29. | (U) | Moore Report, pg 15. |
| 30. | (U) | APG History, Jul 66-Sep 67 pg 16. |
| 31. | (U) | Moore Report, pg 15. |
| 32. | (S) | McLaughlin Interview. |
| 33. | (U)<br>(U)<br><br><br>(U) | APG History, Jul 66-Sep 67, pg 35;<br>Ltr, Major Melvin H. Reed, USAF, Commander, Det 1, 14th Aerial Port Squadron to Commander 14th Aerial Port Squadron, subj: Non-Utilization of Pallet Dollies, 3 Oct 67;<br>Ltr, Brig Gen Burl W. McLaughlin, USAF, Commander, 834th AD to 14th ACW, subj: Ramp Condition, 30 Nov 67. |
| 34. | (U) | Stevenson Report, pg 13. |
| 35. | | <u>Ibid</u>, pg 13. |
| 36. | (U) | Ltr, Brig Gen Hugh E. Wild, USAF, Comdr, 834th AD to 366th TFW, subj: Ramp Congestion, 23 Nov 67. |
| 37. | (S) | Phillips Interview, pg 9. |
| 38. | (S) | 315th AD History, Jan-Dec 66, pg 44. |
| 39. | (U) | Ltr, 7AF to PACAF, subj: Seat Pallets, 4 Jan 68. |
| 40. | (U) | Interview, Capt David Muench, USAF, TACC, TAC, 4 May 69. |

| | | |
|---|---|---|
| 41. | (U) | Logan Interview. |
| 42. | (U) | AFM 2-4, "Tactical Air Force Operations, Tactical Airlift", Wash D.C., DAF, 10 Aug 66. |
| 43. | (U) | APG History, Jul 66-Sep 67, pg 6. |
| 44. | (S) | Command Statistics Rprts, Hq 7AF, Jul-Dec 68. |
| 45. | (S) | TAPA Rprt, Jul 66-Dec 68. |
| 46. | (U) | Whitney Interview. |

## CHAPTER V

| | | |
|---|---|---|
| 1. | (S/AFEO) | End-of-Tour Report, Maj Gen Burl W. McLaughlin, USAF, Comdr, 834th AD, Nov 67 to Jun 69, Chapter 3, p. 1. (Hereafter cited: General McLaughlin End of Tour Rprt.) |
| 2. | | Ibid. |
| 3. | (S) | Ltr, Maj Gen Burl W. McLaughlin, USAF, Comdr, 834th AD, subj: CHECO Report Coordination, Atch 2, pg 2. |
| 4. | | General McLaughlin, End-of-Tour Rprt, pg 2. |
| 5. | | Ibid. |
| 6. | (U) | End-of-Tour Report, Col J. J. Schneider, USAF, Comdr, Det 1, 834th AD, Aug 68-May 69, pg 12; Interview, Lt Col Ben H. Varner, DCM, 135th SOW, 6 May 69; |
| | (U) | Stevenson Report, 7. |
| | (U) | IG Report 68, pg N3. |

## GLOSSARY

| | |
|---|---|
| ACL | Allowable Cabin Load |
| ACS | Air Commando Squadron |
| AFLC | Air Force Logistics Command |
| AGE | Aerospace Ground Equipment |
| ALCC | Airlift Control Center |
| ALCE | Airlift Control Element |
| ALOC | Air Line of Communications |
| ARC | Aerospace Research Corporation |
| ARVN | Army of Republic of Vietnam |
| ATC | Air Traffic Control |
| AUTODIN | Automatic Digital Network |
| AWCC | Artillery Warning and Control Center |
| | |
| CARP | Computed Air Release Point |
| CCT | Combat Control Team |
| CDS | Container Delivery System |
| CE | Combat Essential |
| CEA | Circular Error Average |
| CINCPAC | Commander-in-Chief, Pacific Command |
| CONUS | Continental United States |
| CRC | Combat Reporting Center |
| CSA | Chief of Staff, United States Army |
| | |
| DASC | Direct Air Support Center |
| Det | Detachment |
| DIFM | Due in from Maintenance |
| DZ | Drop Zone |
| | |
| ER | Emergency Resupply |
| EZ | Extraction Zone |
| | |
| FAC | Forward Air Controller |
| FM | Frequency Modulation |
| | |
| GCA | Ground Controlled Approach |
| GPES | Ground Proximity Extraction System |
| | |
| HF | High Frequency |
| | |
| ILS | Instrument Landing System |
| IMC | Instrument Meteorological Conditions |
| IRAN | Inspection and Repair as Necessary |
| | |
| LAPES | Low Altitude Parachute Extraction System |
| LIT | Light Intratheater Transport |

| | |
|---|---|
| MAC | Military Airlift Command |
| MACV | Military Assistance Command, Vietnam |
| Med-evac | Medical Evacuation |
| MHE | Materials Handling Equipment |
| | |
| NCO | Noncommissioned Officer |
| NORS | Not Operationally Ready-Supply |
| NVN | North Vietnamese |
| | |
| OHR | Operational Hazard Report |
| OJT | On-the-Job Training |
| OR | Operationally Ready |
| OSD | Office of the Secretary of Defense |
| | |
| PACAF | Pacific Air Forces |
| PCS | Permanent Change of Station |
| PSP | Pierced Steel Planking |
| | |
| RDD | Required Delivery Date |
| RTAF | Royal Thai Air Force |
| | |
| SAC | Strategic Air Command |
| SEAOR | Southeast Asia Operational Requirement |
| SKT | Specialty Knowledge Test |
| SOS | Special Operations Squadron |
| SOW | Special Operations Wing |
| STOL | Short Take Off and Landing |
| | |
| TAC | Tactical Air Command |
| TACAN | Tactical Air Navigation |
| TACC | Tactical Air Control Center |
| TACP | Tactical Air Control Party |
| TALO | Tactical Airlift Liaison Officer |
| TAPA | Tactical Airlift Performance Accomplishments |
| TAW | Tactical Airlift Wing |
| TCTO | Time Compliance Technical Orders |
| TDY | Temporary Duty |
| TE | Tactical Emergency |
| TMA | Transportation Management Agency |
| TO | Technical Order |
| TUOC | Tactical Unit Operations Center |
| | |
| UHF | Ultra High Frequency |
| UMD | Unit Manning Document |
| UNAAF | Unified Action Armed Forces |
| USARV | United States Army, Vietnam |

| | |
|---|---|
| VHF | Very High Frequency |
| VMC | Visual Meteorological Conditions |
| VNAF | Vietnamese Air Force |
| VTOL | Vertical Take Off and Landing |
| WRAMA | Warner Robins Air Materiel Area |

Declassified IAW E.O. 12958
Air Force Declassification Office and
Approved for Public Release.
Date: 8-15-06

DECLASSIFIED

www.ingramcontent.com/pod-product-compliance
Lightning Source LLC
Chambersburg PA
CBHW080544170426
43195CB00016B/2676